LET'S GO FISHING!

*Come, so we go
to conquer all!*
Nov. 2022

Evangelist Carol J. Pryor

LET'S GO FISHING!
Copyright © 2022 by Evangelist Carol J. Pryor

Library of Congress Control Number: 2021924442
ISBN-13:   Paperback: 978-1-64674-171-7
            ePub: 978-1-64674-172-4

Printed in the United States of America

LitFire
PUBLISHING
LitFire LLC
1-800-511-9787
www.litfirepublishing.com
order@litfirepublishing.com

Contents

*To my parents, the Late Minister Willis G.
and Mother Flora B. Pryor*

*To my siblings, the Late Alfred W., Bishop Marvin C.
& Doris L. Pryor*

To the following:

The Pryor & Lee Ethel Ellis Family

Pastor & Evangelist Walter T. Pryor

Supt. Chris V. (Kenyatta) Pryor

Mo. Isabella Calhoun

The Late Supervisor Earlie M, Peppers,

*Cousin Versie Humes, Missionary Jeanette E. Jones, Missionary
Claudette Hunt, Brother Sidney Oliver, Mrs. Willa Hawkins,
Southwest Michigan Third Ecclesiastical Jurisdiction*

Victorious Believers Ministries COGIC, Michigan

Aden Rock Godson

In Memoriam

Bishop Marvin C. Pryor, Chief Prasier

Sunrise: October 26, 1940 – Sunset: February 22, 2010

So he fed them according to the integrity of his heart; and guided them by the skillfulness of his hands...

Bishop Marvin C. Pryor, a scholar, a gentleman, a saint...

The Shepherd of our fold has laid down his staff and transitioned beyond the reach of mortal man. On Monday, February 22, 2010, he beheld the light that beckoned him from earth to glory and answered the call. Again, it has pleased the Supreme Architect of the universe in His infinite wisdom to call from labor to reward our loved one, **Bishop Marvin C. Pryor.**

The Early Years

Bishop Marvin C. Pryor was born October 26, 1940 in Villa Ridge, Illinois (Pryor Town), the fifth of nine children born to the union of the late Deacon and Mother Willis (Flora) Pryor, Sr. Bishop Pryor was a third generation Church of God in Christ son. His grandfather founded Villa Ridge Church of God in Christ (currently Pryor Memorial COGIC) in 1917. As a child, his parents trained and nourished him in the admonition of the Lord and Godly principles. They also inspired him to excel in education and challenged him "to get your learning, but don't lose your burning" for the things of God.

The Pryor family relocated to Jackson, Michigan in his early childhood. In April 1951, he accepted Jesus Christ as his Lord and Savior at the age of 10 years old. In that same night he received the baptism of the Holy Ghost and remained committed to Christ and the church throughout his entire life. Throughout his academic and career trail he always put God first. Bishop Pryor often quoted St. Matthew 6:33, *"But seek ye first, the kingdom of God and his righteousness and all these things shall be added unto you"* and *"Salvation + Education = Success"*.

A Scholarly Man

He was educated in the Jackson Public School system and graduated from Jackson High School in 1958. He pursued academic studies at Michigan State University, earning a Bachelor of Arts degree in Political Science and History. He continued his studies at The University of Michigan-Ann Arbor, earning a Master of Arts degree in Guidance and Counseling and doctoral studies in Educational Leadership and Administration.

A Man of Service

Bishop Pryor was a retired thirty (30) year Educator in the Flint Public School system. He loved working with youth and his peers. He was down-to-earth, relatable, youth-oriented and a sharp thinker. Students easily embraced his genuine and transparent nature. During his extensive career in education he served a few years as a school teacher and guidance counselor. He was the city's first African American guidance counselor. His gift of administration catapult his promotion as a twenty-four (24) year school administrator - junior high school assistant principal and principal of Holmes Junior High. He also completed special work assignments by the school district as a contract negotiator and served as Assistant Pupil Personnel Director at the Administration Building. In 1976, he was appointed principal of the largest high school in the county, Flint Northern High School, "Home of the Champions." As a principal, he was not only intricately involved in the student's and staff success, but he was a avid supporter of the school's extracurricular programs and could be seen on campus or across the state almost any day cheering on his Flint Northern Vikings. During his tenure he hosted several international dignitaries such as: President Jimmy Carter, Vice-President Walter Mondale and cultural icon Muhammad Ali among others.

A Godly Servant

Bishop Pryor accepted his call to the ministry on December 25, 1966, received his minister's license in 1967 and was ordained and Elder in the Church of God in Christ in 1972. As a churchman, Bishop Pryor served loyally and faithfully as a member, administrator and associate elder of Greater Holy Temple Church of God in Christ under the leadership of Elder Roger L. Jones (currently Bishop of Southeast Michigan Jurisdiction) from 1964 to 1984. Because of his unyielding service, Bishop Jones recommended Bishop Pryor for the pastorate to another local assembly. It was God's plan to expand Bishop Pryor's service beyond the Flint area when he was appointed pastor of Williams Memorial Church of God in Christ, Saginaw (currently Victorious Believers Ministries Church of God inChrist) in 1984 by the late Presiding Bishop J.O. Patterson, Sr. (at the demise of jurisdictional prelate, Bishop John Seth Bailey).

Bishop Pryor accepted early retirement in 1992 to accommodate the growth of his local church ministry and to commit further to the work of the ministry at home and abroad, including community service in the Great Lakes Bay region. He advised and worked with diverse leaders in the community on various issues of social change and enhancement for our community. He was a member of Governor Jennifer Granholm's Faith-Based Initative Board. Governor Granholm cited Bishop Pryor as *"a dedicated leader and community activist who was selfless in his missionary work at home and around the world. As a member of my Clergy Leadership Advisory Council, he was a trusted advisor to me and a partner in our effort to forge faith-based and neighborhood partnerships."*

exceeded any man's ability to take care of it all, Bishop Pryor was committed to give as much of himself and his time to help make a difference. He served the ecumenical and secular communities collectively for forty-eight (48) years as an educator, spiritual advisor, mentor, pastor, bridge-builder, bishop, motivator and friend. The central theme of his ministry at Victorious Believers Ministries (VBM) was to empower everyday people for victorious living. *Victorious Living is a way of life!* Under Bishop Pryor's ministry, Believers were challenged to walk not in defeat, but inspired to walk in victory, according to I Corinthians 15:57 & II Corinthians 2:14, *But thanks be to God, who gives us the victory through our Lord Jesus Christ and causes us to triumph and make manifest the savior of his knowledge by us in every place.*

At VBM, Bishop Pryor was the Chief Praiser. He was an anointed man of God and preacher who believed in giving God glory and often admonished the saints, *"Oh, bless His name"* which was a clarion call for the congregation to shout unto God with a voice of triumph. Under his leadership the church grew exponentially by converting and training believers for the work of the ministry. In 1999, VBM built and reloctaed to its present facility, a 50,000 square feet multi-purpose edifice comprising a worship center, administrative center and Family Life Center. VBM provided more than seventy (70) diverse Inreach and Outreach ministries and services to members and the community of all ages and across socio-economics backgrounds. Bishop Pryor often proclaimed, *"if the church isn't for everybody than it isn't for anybody."* With that in mind, the church adapted one of its slogans as "Impacting the Lives of Everyday People." Bishop Pryor believed that the gospel of Jesus Christ could change anyone and that the church should be a impacting body of believers to maximize their potential naturally and spiritually. Bishop Pryor also promoted a "Spirit of Excellence in Holiness" as the ministry's philosophy.

VBM and Bishop Pryor's mission outreach extended beyond its locality and supports ministries and missionaries in South Africa, Trinidad, Haiti, other foreign fields and disaster relief funds within the United States. On the night of his passing, Bishop Pryor had just returned from a seven (7) day mission trip in Burkina Faso, Africia with Compassion Internationl Ministries. The church's 501c3 faith-based corporation, VBM Community Outreach, Incorporated (VBMCO) was established in 1999 and offers local, state, federal and privately-funded programs and activities to empower everyday people for purposeful & development, health and educational programs in the Family Life Center. The church also operates a HUD-certified housing counseling agency, Victory Resource Center.

On May 9, 1996, Bishop Pryor was elevated to episcopacy of the Church of God in Christ. He was apponited jurisdictional bishop of The Third Ecclesiastical Jurisdiction Southwest Michigan by former Presiding Bishop Chandler David Owens. As a pace-setting leader and church builder, Bishop Pryor provided oversight and exemplary leadership for pastors and churches of this ecclesiastical body in Saginaw, Flint, Lansing, Ann Arbor, Detroit, Grand Rapids, Kalamazoo and South Haven. Within the national church Bishop Pryor served in various capacities. In 1995 he was appointed by Presiding Bishop Owens to serve as a facilitator on the Presiding Bishop's 2000 & Beyond Church Growth Team as they began preparing pastors and leaders for the twenty-first century. From 2000-2005, the late Presiding Bishop G.E. Patterson appointed Bishop Pryor as the National Director of Church Growth & Development. In 2009, Presiding Bishop C.E. Blake appointed him as a governing board member of the Church of God in Christ Publishing House Board.

A Family Man

On August 18, 1963 he united in holy matrimony with the love of his life who sparked the twinkle in his eye, Ruth C. Trice of Jackson. She was his prized jewel and help-mete. She was an anointed young singer who loved the Lord with all her heart. They became one in mind, heart and soul with a bond and love that would last forever and supersede the boundaries of marriage into their ministry. They continued their spiritual legacy by raising four children in the fear and admonition of the Lord. The church, his family and his God were his life. Bishop Pryor was bestowed the honor of "Father of the Year" by former Mayor. City of Flint, Woodrow Stanley.

He leaves to treasure his memory and continue his legacy to his devoted wife and co-laborer of over forty-six (46) years. Evangelist Ruth C. Pryor and his loving children, Derrick, Missionary Vonda, Elder Mel and Elder Christopher Pryor; two daughter in laws, Gwendolyn and Kenyatta; four grandchildren; Alexis, Loren, Carrington and Chandler; his siblings; Mrs. Lee Ethel (John) Ellis, Deacon Willis Pryor, Jr., Pastor Walter (Jackie) Pryor, Evangelist Carol J. Pryor and Mr. David Pryor; special nieces: Tracy. Stacey and Kym Pryor; many cousins, nieces, nephews; other relatives and friends to include the members of Victorious Believers Ministries Church of God in Christ; The Third Ecclesiastical Jurisdiction Southwest Michigan; Presiding Bishop Charles E. Blake and the entire Church of God in Christ worldwide and those whose lives are richer because he lived and served.

His life's motto was: *I can do all things through Christ which strengthen me.* Philippians 4:13.

FOREWORD

I have worked with Evangelist Carol Jean Pryor for approximately for 25 years in the field of evangelism. I admire her positive approach to life and all life throws at her.

The book is the ultimate inside look at evangelism and should be on the desk of every pastor and evangelist who wants evangelism as a part of their organization.

Evangelist Pryor's approach to Evangelism is inherently process driven, rather than filled with a lot of "thou shalt nots." As a result this book is remarkably thorough, smartly written and incredibly helpful.

Evangelist Pryor has spent countless hours helping other organizations with their evangelistic department. You will be glad to have the author's experience as you plan and implement your organization's evangelism department.

Evangelist Pryor would make herself available to churches and organizations that would contact her for presentations and workshops for hands on assistance.

Missionary Jeanette Elaine Jones
Founder of Golden Seniors Ministry

WORDS FROM THE AUTHOR

This book was written out of my heart and experiences serving under the leadership of my brother, pastor, and bishop, the late Marvin C. Pryor. Even though he has made his transition to heaven, his life has left an impact that will never be erased or forgotten.

The information shared is not theory but written from the brainstorming, planning, services, events, and regular staff sessions conducted at Victorious Believers Ministries Church of God in Christ from Saginaw, Michigan. In October of 2012, nearly four months prior to his death, Bishop Marvin C. Pryor celebrated twenty-five years as pastor of the church. I was blessed and honored to have been involved during most of that time. The church name was Williams Memorial COGIC, but by the end of his life, the vision had reflected his purpose on earth, so being changed to Victorious Believers Ministries (VBM). He and his wife, Evangelist Ruth C. Pryor, lead us from "Catch the Vision" to the "Vision Unfolds!" to "Run with the Vision!"

Pastor Pryor made the decision to change the name of the church from Williams Memorial to what is now called Victorious Believers Ministries (VBM). He chose a name to reflect the vision for the ministry and would stimulate each member to live *victoriously*, no matter circumstances!

I served as the Director of Evangelism at the local church. It was one of my responsibilities to encourage members to do *personal evangelism, one on one contact and* corporate outreach's efforts; which extend to the masses extending throughout the world.

VBM is yet working at fulfilling the vision, even though Bishop Pryor, is no longer present to guide. His son, Pastor Christopher V. Pryor, is directing and mandating the outreach of the ministry.

INTRODUCTION

Let's Go Fishing!
Deputize to Evangelize

Evangelism is the practice of zealously preaching and spreading the gospel or good news of Jesus Christ through witnessing individually or corporate outreach. Building a structured evangelism program in our church helps us to know *where* we are going and *how* we are growing. Evangelism is discussed much but explained little in most of our church world in the 21st century. Another definition for evangelism is to gossip the good news of our deliverance from sin by Jesus the Savior with unbelievers, as stated in *Acts 8:4: "Therefore those who were scattered went everywhere preaching the word."*

The reasons why pastors are often unexcited, uninvolved, and unsuccessful in evangelism is because we concentrate on telling the "good news" to saints rather than to sinners. "Our congregations need to be more aware of, and involved with the unbelieving world around them." In order to build this awareness, evangelism should have top priority in all membership, discipleship, and department/ministry training objectives and written materials.

When planning special events, we should always ask *how* this activity relates to the unbeliever. When churches present a fiscal budget, local and foreign missions must be priority item. If we are not budgeting to purchase or print outreach materials, if we are not meeting people's needs and promoting Christ outside of the church, if we are not pushing for growth wherever possible, our leadership will not be aware of evangelism's importance to the overall church program. *There is no growing without setting goals in giving of finances and time, going out on a continual basis, and discipling new converts.* It can be defined as an evangelism program when the total church are trained to witness and follow-up occurs.

The Bible declares that there is not a lack of sinners but a need for more soul winners; *"Therefore pray the Lord of the harvest to send out laborers into His harvest" (Matthew 9:38).* Every leader within a church, as well as members in the pews should walk with Jesus through His methodology on building the awareness of evangelism's priority through leadership and expectation of the pastor. Rather, daily evangelism as a one-on-one examples of Christ witnesses to the woman at the well in *John 4:1-26;* Christ witnesses to Nicodemus in *John 3:1-21;* or Philip witnesses to Egyptian eunuch in *Acts 8:6-40.* The corporate or church evangelism program, as shared in *Acts 2:36-41, Peter explain Pentecost, and nearly 3,000 souls were added to the church.*

Pulpit preaching alone doesn't change families, communities, cities or world, but *committed* people sitting in the pews, and they do it by announcing Jesus and invite others to know Him in a clear and positive way daily. As the body of Christ, our normal "proclamation days" center around holidays, revivals, concerts, missions, or special well-known guest speakers as what can be called corporate evangelism. Churches aren't using these methods as frequent as before the 21st century. Building relationships with unbelievers in every possible avenue of respectable community life demonstrates our loving concern for people.

In our local assemblies, we must evaluate and maintain "acceptance" of all people throughout our communities, regardless of race, color or nationality. Believers must pray for open eyes, hearts, and minds of unbelievers and backsliders (Matthew 9:30). *When someone accepts Christ, be ready to accept them!*

Everyday Evangelism Outreach/Personal Soul Winning

Deputize to Evangelize

The Mission:
Evangelism—having to do with (purposely) reaching out to people with the good news of Jesus Christ, to convert or compel them to accept and become a new creature in Him; a Soul Winner through gatherings through the means of revivals or crusades or one on one contacts.

Scriptural Calling to Serve:
Deputize—empowerment, potentiality, force, mightiness, vitality, vigor, vim, push, drive, or charge.

The Call to Evangelize:
Then He said to them, "Follow Me, and I will make you fishers of men" (Matthew 4:19)

Models of evangelizing in Matthew 22: 1–14; Luke 14: 16–23

"You are the light of the world. A city that is set on a hill cannot be hidden. Not do they light a lamp and put it under a basket, but on a lampstand, and it gives light to all who are in the house. Let your light so shine before men, that they may see your good works and glorify your Father in heaven" (Matthew 5:14-16)

"Go ye therefore, and preach all nations, baptizing them in the name of Father; and of the Son, and of the Holy Ghost: Teaching them to observe all things whatsoever I have commanded you: and, lo I am with you always, even unto the end of the world. Amen" (Matthew 28:19–20)

"And I, if I am lifted up from the earth, will draw all men unto me" (John 12:32)

"Verily, verily, I say unto you. He that believeth on me, the works that I do shall he do also; and greater works than these shall he do, that the Father may be glorified in the Son" (John 14:12)

"But ye shall receive power after the Holy Ghost comes upon you; and ye shall be witnesses unto me both in Jerusalem, and in all Judea, and in Samaria, and unto the uttermost part of the earth" (Acts 1:8)

"But in your hearts set Christ apart as holy [and acknowledge Him] as Lord. Always be ready to give a logical defense to anyone who asks you to account for the hope that is in you, but do it courteously and respectively" (1 Peter 3:15)

Witness—a person who can give firsthand account of something seen or heard or experienced; attest, give evidence to disclose or vouch, states one case. A witness can avow, or confirm that either person or that stated.

Factor #1: *Deputized*

—To appoint or serve as a deputy or empowered to act in place of or for another to achieve a task or assignment with authority.

Heed the *Call* to Evangelize:

Every Soul Winner or convert from sin to Salvation should know their role to win Souls by spreading of the Gospel (good news of Jesus Christ), through the *message and testimony* with love and passion. Read Ephesians 6: 19 and 20 as your "confession" to serve as a Soul Winner.

Authorization
Wear Your Armor

Read Ephesians 6:10–20

"Finally, my brethren, be strong in the Lord, and in the power of his might. Put on the whole armour of God, that ye may be able to stand against the wiles of the devil. For we wrestle not against flesh and blood, but against principalities, against powers, against rulers of darkness of this world, against spiritual wickedness in high places. Wherefore take unto you the whole armour of God, that ye may be able to withstand in the evil day, and having done all, to stand. Stand therefore, having your loins girt about with truth, and having on the breastplate of righteousness; And your feet shod with the preparation of the gospel of peace; Above all, taking the shield of faith, wherewith ye shall be able approach all the fiery darts of the wicked. And take the helmet of salvation, and the sword of the Spirit, which is the word of God: Praying always with all prayer and supplication in the Spirit, and watching thereunto with all perseverance and supplication for all saints;

And for me, that utterance may be given unto me, that I may open my mouth boldly, to make known the mystery of the gospel. For which I am an ambassador in bonds: that herein I may speak boldly , as I ought to speak."

The Great Commission, Soul Winning is a Command

"Go ye therefore, and teach all nations, baptizing them in the name of the Father, and of the Son, and of the Holy Ghost" (Matt. 28:19, KJV)

"Go out and train everyone you meet, far and near, in this way of life, marking them by baptism in the threefold name: Father, Son, and Holy Spirit. Then instruct them in the practice of all I have commanded you. I'll be with you as you do this, day after day, right up to end of the age."

(Matt. 28:19, Message Bible)

Checklist for Daily Living (Romans 12: 1-21; I Thessalonians 5:12-22)

__Respect those who teach and guide you in the Lord's ways.
__Live in peace with others.
__Encourage those who are timid.
__Help and encourage the weak.
__Pray at all times.
__Be patient with everyone.
__Be thankful in every situation.
__Always be joyful.
__Take to heart that which is good.
__Do not take lightly what God has said.
__Stay away from every kind of evil.

__Make sure that what you believe agrees with God's Word.

__Guard your mouth and the flame of God's Spirit in your heart.

__Read various scriptures and meditate on God's Word. (Ex.: Proverbs for daily living situations)

Factor #2: *The Bait*

Let's Go Fishing!
Day-to-Day Reaching Out
Acts of Witnessing

Listed are *ways* that as an individual, as a family, two by two or with a team of individuals can witness regarding the death, burial, and resurrection of Jesus Christ as soul winners and draw men, women, boys and girls to be restored by spreading of the gospel through witnessing, which causes repentance; forgiveness of sin and adding of souls to the kingdom of God daily.

Evangelism has everything to do with spreading the message of Jesus Christ (through your testimony or personal account of conversion in your life) to every person, neighborhood, city, and state. The effectiveness of these *ways* have a profound impact upon the nation and reaches throughout to the world.

We are God's tools to either compel, "fetch", "draw", and "bring" people to a point of commitment to Jesus Christ as Lord and Savior. We are to "take away" men's souls from the enemy and receive them in Jesus Christ.

The Word of God:

1. Make sure family members are taught the story of Jesus' birth, life, death, burial, and resurrection.
   Read Matthew, Mark, Luke, John and the Acts

2. Memorize scriptures that are used to cause individuals to accept Jesus as Lord.
   Romans 3:23 *"For all have sinned, and come short of the glory of God."*

Other biblical words for sin:

Disobedience (Rom. 5:19; Col. 3:6; Heb. 2:2)
Fault (Deut. 25:2; I Pet. 7:20)
Error (Jas 5:20; 2 Pet. 2:18; 3:17)
Transgression (Rom. 4:15; I Jn. 3:4)
Ungodliness (Rom. 1:18, 2 Tim. 2:16; Tit. 2:12)
Unrighteousness (Rom. 1:29; I Jn 1:9; 5:17)
Inequity (Acts 3:26; Rom. 4:7; Tit. 2:14)
Offense (Eccl. 10:4; Rom. 5:15-20; 2 Cor. 11:7)

"I have not come to call the righteous, but sinners, to repentance." Luke 5:32

A Christian's attitude toward sin:

Read *Ps. 97:10; Prov. 6:16-19; Am. 5:15; John 3:16; I Thess. 5:22; Rom. 5:8; Rom. 6:1, 2, 12; I John 1–5*

1. We should hate sin, not the sinner.
2. We should lay it aside.
3. We should abstain from sin.

4. Never be judgmental and watch the look of disapproval, rebuke, disdain, superiority, condemnation.

5. Maintain the expression of God's love. *"Yes, I have loved thee with an everlasting love: therefore with lovingkindness have I drawn thee" (Jeremiah 31:3, KJV)*

6. Learn to "handle" rejections regardless of (negative) responses.

Factor #3: *The Fish*

The Method and Message to Witnessing; Soul Winning Strategies and Evangelizing Techniques:

1. Your testimony.

   (Suggestion: Write out your story of conversion. Answer *how, who, when, what, and where.*) Summarize. ____

   Saved, Holy Ghost filled, sanctified, set aside for service.

   A. Christ came into your life (Romans 10: 9, 10, 13; Revelation 3:20).

   B. Your sins were forgiven (I John 1:9)

   C. You became a child of God (John 1:12)

   D. You received eternal life (John 3:16).

   E. You began the great adventure for which God created you (2 Corinthians 5:17).

   F. You have become a greater witness (Acts 1:8)

   G. Keep your testimony *"powerful, fresh, and anointed"* by reflecting and thankful.

2. Pray daily before interacting with people, asking God to direct as you approach individuals in your pathway. Let the light of Christ shine! ____

"You are the light of the world, A city that is set on a hill cannot be hidden...Let your light so shine before men, that they may see your good works and glorify your Father in heaven" (Matthew 5:14, 16)

"Then Jesus spoke to them again, saying, 'I am the light of the world. He who follows Me shall not walk in darkness, but have the light of life'" (John 8:32)

"While you have the light, believe in the light, that you may become 'sons of light'"

(John 12:36)
"And I, if I be lifted up from the earth, will draw all men unto me" (John 12:32)

3. Make sure through prayer, study the Word of God, and meditating *daily* to keep your flesh under submission, *"Let your speech always be with grace, seasoned with salt, that you may know how you ought to answer each one." Col. 3:6* (Read Col. 4:2-6) ____

4. Teach and by example, instruct your family members that their actions must reflect the life of holiness: Holiness in Family Life (Col. 3:18-21) and Holiness in Work Life (Col. 3:22-25) ____

5. "Adopt" a family from within the neighborhood to provide needs, until they become self-sufficient through personal or church provision. ____

6. Volunteer as a Big Sister or Big Brother through the means of social programs.____

7. Become a Pen Pal to someone in prison or armed forces. ____

8. "Adopt" Senior Citizen(s) to call, visit, and/or provide as needed weekly. ____

9. Regularly visit either hospitals, convalescent, or nursing homes as a volunteer. ____

10. Collect clothing, furniture, food and toys throughout the year, especially during Christmas. ____

11. Join a team of believers that will pray for the surroundings regarding peace and order in neighborhoods. ____

12. Become a member of your child's parent associations at schools. Attend school activities, including report card pick-ups, and connect with staff. Volunteer for lunch room duty. If permitted at school, volunteer as classroom(s) helper. ____

13. Volunteer at a Men's or Women's shelters. ____

14. Leave a generous tip with a tract or media card inviting to church at a restaurant. ____

15. Mail greeting cards or tracts, or media cards to family, friends, and co-workers for birthdays, holidays or anniversaries. ____

16. Emergency situations broadcasted on televisions, and radio that you can respond by prayer, donations, and cards to express concerns. ____

17. Donate to foreign missions to fulfill requests through your local church or outreach services. ____

18. Use greetings, smiles, and hugs to show the love of God. ____

19. Invite or bring individuals to church, especially to activities/events sponsored by church. ____

20. Volunteer to serve the Meals on Wheels Program in your city. ____

21. Build a "bridge" or connect to Backsliders (Jeremiah 3:14). ____

22. Collect Bibles, religious books, CDs and DVDs to distribute to family, friends, and coworkers. ____

23. Wear T-shirts that has scripture and wording to relay message of God's love and identify church name. ____

24. Before arriving at destination, ask God through Jesus, to allow the Holy Spirit to use you to witness and draw to Himself. ____

Teamwork Evangelism:

> 25. Believers connected two by two or more to form evangelistic opportunities to witness through social gatherings or outings on a weekly basis. _____ (Consider sporting events, picnics, walks, exercising/ fitness gyms, recreational outings.)

Launch out in the "Deep":

> 26. Form a team that will regularly reach out to Downtown Houston to witness and provide a "love gift" of a packaged meal, tract on Salvation, media card about church and how to attend. (Ex. Inform them that transport by Metro to Greenspoint Mall Station, and drop off and pickup by HTCs van shuttle is available.)

Use of Social Media techniques or tools provided by church on a weekly schedule:

Use of social church on a weekly schedule:

> 27. Use of Social Media: Emails, Text, Facebook, Link, and Tweet Messages, place posters about church and church events wherever free bulletin boards made available. Ask each family to place fliers or posters on the bulletin board to announce your local church to invite to services and/or special events.

> 28. Children Evangelism techniques during family outings, school attendance, and at play with friends using (conversations and behaviors) that cause responses versus reactions.

"Train up a child in the way he should go, And when he is old he will not depart from it" (Proverbs 22:6)

29. Weekly Corporate Evangelism:

It is important that every member of the local church, rather weeknights or Sunday services understand their *passionate* participation during services is absolutely necessary as they sit in whatever section of the church. ____

A. Before service begin, greet those in the sanctuary as you approach your choice of seating.

B. Connect with smiles/hugs to those in your section.

C. Participate during Praise and Worship actively, and encourage your children to become worshippers.

D. When the Altar Call is made, pray and be willing to walk to the front with someone responding.

E. Follow up contact is necessary on behalf of new convert.

F. Sign up, at least once a month, to your church's weekly evangelism department to Witness/ SWAT (Soul Winning Across Town) Ministry. Bishop Bob Jackson & ACTS of Full Gospel COGIC, Oakland, Ca

30. Exchange names amongst members to reach out to family, friends, associates, and coworkers distributing CDs, media cards, tracks, invitations to events and activities on a weekly basis.

Evangelism Buzz Words and Phrases:

New Testament words

Disciple	A follower of Jesus.
Evangelist	A person who tells others the Good News of Jesus, known as the Gospel.
Fellowship	A close friendship between two or more people.
Flesh	Our physical bodies and the sinful nature in us.
Gospel	The Good News that Jesus saves us from sin.
Grace	Free, undeserved forgiveness and favor.
Intercede	Praying for someone in need as if that person were praying.
Pastor	The leader of a church. He is a shepherd of God's people.
Perish	To die and be separated from God forever.
Reconcile	To make a relationship right. To make peace with someone.
Redeem	To buy back something that one owned, or to pay for someone to be free.
Repent	To ask for forgiveness and turn from sin.
Righteous	Completely right, good, fair and sinless.
Saint	Someone who made holy by God and chosen to serve Him. Every believer is a saint.
Salvation	Being saved from sin and eternal punishment.
Sanctify	To make holy and pure (free from sin).
[Be] Saved	To be a child of God and have eternal life.
Scripture	The Bible; God's written Word
Soul	The part inside us that thinks, chooses to do right or wrong and feels emotions.
Spirit	The unseen part of us that lives forever and connects us with God.

Temple   The House of God; a place of worship; the church building.

Witness   To show people that you follow Jesus and tell them about God's love.

Ordinary People by Age Group

Senior Adults
(born early 1900s)
   The Baby Boomer Generation
The Millennials (21st Century)
    Youth (teens)
    Children

Ordinary People by Relationship Group

Family
(married, single or divorced)
   Friends
   Coworkers
   Neighbors
   Classmates
   Strangers
   Diversity

Ordinary People by Life Situation

Abuse Victims
Addicts
Convicts
People Affected by Disability
The Homeless
*Millennials

The Affluent
The Poor
The Unemployed
The Outcasts

Ordinary People by Race

African American
Asians
Caucasians
Hispanic
Native American

Ordinary People by Religion

Agnostics

Recent Immigrants

International Students

Summary of Day-to-Day Evangelism Results
Building Blocks as Strategies for Winning the Lost

Building Block #1: Awareness

Building a structured evangelism program in a church helps to know where it's going and how a church (HTC) is growing. Evangelism must be discussed, explained, and practiced to promote the need of *awareness*, our congregations must know the definition of evangelism, how to approach the unbeliever, lead the unbeliever to Christ anytime and anywhere. In order to build this *awareness*, evangelism should have top priority in all membership, discipleship, and departmental training objectives and provided written materials. Meeting the needs of people, spiritually and naturally, promoting Christ outside of the church; there is no growing without setting goals in giving and going.

Building Block #2: Announcement

We must *announce* the good news, called the Gospel, to everyone within our families, friends, coworkers, communities, states, and throughout the world. Pulpit preaching is not enough to reach out, but one on one does it part to *announce* Jesus and inviting others to know Him in a clear and positive way! Within the church, normal "proclamation days" center when certain holidays on calendar, revivals, conferences, mission outreach activities, special occasions or guest speakers (annually) scheduled. Discussion and strategies must be developed to effectively reach children, high school and college students, factory workers, special-interest groups, socioeconomic, and social-issues groups, government officials, sports teams, community and VIP's, and the general populous that live around the church. Building relationships with unbelievers in every possible avenue of respectable community life demonstrates our loving concern for people as an individual or as a church as believers.

Building Block #3: Acceptance

As motivated, aware leadership and laity continuously and thoroughly announce Christ, many begin to "accept" Him as Christ whenever the *people become aware of the good news as announced and acceptance* is the outcome from our efforts to evangelize. Evaluating outreach effectiveness can be concluded from how it is reported as in the New Testament through signs and wonders (John 2:11), numbers counted (Acts 2:41); through reports given to leadership, and through seeing them added to the church (Acts 2:47). Evangelistic decisions or initial acceptance does not constitute effectiveness. True "acceptance" of the Gospel must turn into affirmation of what Christ has done and is doing in someone's life (Acts 2:44-46). Acceptance can be assessed as "front door, back door syndrome meaning Numbers versus Numbers that count". An ongoing discipleship class or new believers must be taught continually, regardless of the number meeting. As we approach the Decade of Harvest, let us be aware , let us identify and plan to announce the Gospel, and let us be ready to accept those who do accept Jesus as Savior!

CHAPTER 1

Two-Fold Ministry of the Church

"And how shall they preach; except they be sent? As it is written, How beautiful are the feet of them that preach the gospel of peace, and bring glad tidings of good things!" (Romans 10:15)

"Come, follow me and I will make you fishers of men" (Mark 1:17)

Scripture Reading:

Matthew 28:19-20
"Go ye therefore, and teach all nations, baptizing them in the name of the Father, and of the Son, and of the Holy Ghost: Teaching them to observe all things whatsoever I have commanded you, and, lo, I am with you always, even unto the end of the world. Amen.

Mark 16:15
"And he said unto them, Go ye into all the world, and preach the gospel to every creature."

John 8:32
"And ye shall know the truth, and the truth shall make you free."

Acts 1:8

"But ye shall receive power, after that the Holy Ghost is come upon you: and ye shall be witnesses unto me both in Jerusalem, and in all Judaea, and in Samaria, and unto the uttermost part of the earth."

I Corinthians 14:3-5, Amplified
"But [on the other hand], the one who prophesies [who interprets the divine will and purpose in inspired preaching and teaching] speaks to men for their up building and constructive spiritual progress and encouragement and consolation. He who speaks in a [strange] tongue edifies and improves himself, but he who prophesies [interpreting the divine will and purpose and teaching with inspiration] edifies and improves the church and promotes growth [in Christian wisdom, piety, holiness, and happiness]. Now I wish that you might all speak in [unknown] tongues, but more especially [I want you] to prophesy (to be inspired to preach and interpret the divine will and purpose). He who prophesies [who is inspired to preach and teach] is greater (more useful and more important) than he who speaks in [unknown] tongues, unless he should interpret [what he says], so that the church may be edified and receive good from it."

II Corinthians 10:8, 13:10
"For though I should boast somewhat more of our authority, which the Lord hath given us for edification, and not for your destruction, I should not be ashamed: Therefore I write these things being absent, lest being present I should use sharpness, according to the power which the Lord hath given me to edification, and not to destruction."

Ephesians 4:11, 12
"And he gave some, apostle; and some, prophets; and some, pastors and teachers; For the perfecting of the saints, for the work of the ministry, for the edifying of the body of Christ:"

Ephesians 4:29
"Let no corrupt communication proceed out of your mouth, but that which is good to the use of edifying, that it may minister grace unto the hearers."

I. Evangelization
Evangelization may be defined as the efforts put forth by the Church for the salvation of men from sin and error. It is the primary mission of the Church. We aren't to wait for the world or sinners to come to where we assemble; but to bring Christ to the world. To preach the Gospel, *the good news about Jesus Christ,* as a witness to all nations and to take out of them a people for Christ's name is the fundamental mission of the Church. Read *Matthew 28:19, 20, Mark 16:15, and Acts 1:8*

II. Edification
Edification may be defined as the building up of the Church in truth and grace. After sinners have been saved, they must be indoctrinated in the truth of the Scriptures and possessed and filled by the Holy Spirit. There are five agencies which contribute to the edification of the Church:
1. The Christian Ministry, *Ephesians 4:11, 12*
   a. Ministerial Gifts, *I Corinthians* 14:3-5
   b. Ministerial Authority, *II Corinthians 10:8, 13:10*
31. The Word of God, *Colossians 3:16, I Peter 2:2, Hebrews 5:12*
   Colossians 3:16
   "Let the word of Christ dwell in you richly in all wisdom, teaching and admonishing one another in psalms and hymns and spiritual songs, singing with grace in your hearts to the Lord."

I Peter 2:2

"As newborn babes, desire the sincere milk of the word, that ye may grow thereby:"

Hebrews 5:12

"For the word of God is quick, and powerful, and sharper than any two edged sword, piercing even to the dividing asunder of soul and spirit, and of the joints and marrow, and a discerner of the thoughts and intents of the heart."

a. The Gospel the Instrument of Edification, *Acts 20:32*

   "And now, brethren, I commend you to God, and to the word of his grace, which is able to build you up, and to give you an inheritance among all of them that are sanctified."

b. All be done to Edification

"Again, think ye that we excuse ourselves unto you? We speak before God in Christ: but we do all things, dearly beloved, for your edifying."

II Corinthians 12: 19

"Let no corrupt communication proceed out of your mouth, but that which is good to the use of edifying, that it may minister grace unto the hearers."

Ephesians 4:29

2. The Holy Spirit, Galatians 5:25, Ephesians 5:18

   "If we live in the Spirit, let us also walk in the Spirit." Galatians 5:25

"And be not drunk with wine, wherein is excess, but be filled with the Spirit."
Ephesians 5:18

3. The Gifts of the Spirit, I Corinthians 12:4-12
    "Now there are diversities of gifts, but the same Spirit. And these are differences of administrations, but the same Lord. And there are diversities of operations, but it is the same God which worketh all in all. But the same manifestation of the Spirit of the Spirit is given to every man to profit withal. For to one is given by the Spirit word of wisdom, to another the word of knowledge by the same Spirit; To another faith by the same Spirit; to another the gifts of healing by the same Spirit;
    To another the working of miracles, to another prophecy; to another discerning of spirits; to another divers kinds of tongues; to another the interpretation of tongues; But all these worketh that one and the selfsame Spirit, dividing to every man severally as he will. For as the body is one, and hath many members, and all the members of that one body, being many, are one body, so also is Christ."

4. The Sacraments or Ordinances, *Matthew 3:13-16; John 13:5-10;*
    I Corinthians 11:24-34
    A ritual or religious act which serves as a channel of God's grace; the Protestants admit to three: baptism, the Lord's Supper and feet washing.

Scripture Reading:

> Romans 12, Your Body as a living sacrifice, for God's glory
>
> I Corinthians 12 and 13, Spiritual Gifts and
> Understanding God's Love
>
> Ephesians 4, Serving as the Body of Christ

A Ministry or Church depends upon Christ, not upon a Man. When one becomes a Christian, Romans 12 says we receive the Mind of Christ, in order that God's will is recognized individually. The Scriptures in Romans 12: 1 says, *"I beseech you therefore, brethren by the mercies of God, that ye present your bodies a living sacrifice, holy, acceptable unto God, which is your reasonable service."*

Also from Romans 12, in regards to Evangelism, verse 9 admonishes the Ministry or Church should *"Let love be without dissimulation. Abhor that which is evil; cleave to that which is good."* In other words, as Christians working together; let our love be sincere for one another so we can be effective as winning souls to the Kingdom.

Romans 12, emphasizes several themes in review:

1. Present your body, be an example of what you speak as expectations for living in this world.
2. Be devoted, committed and consecrated to God individually and collectively as the Body of Christ.
3. For as in the physical body, there are many parts (organs, members) with different functions, we must remember that we are parts of one another [are dependent upon one another.]

4. Each of us have gifts from God, so let us use them as practical service, building one another instead of selfish gain.

I Corinthians 12 and 13, reminds us how to use the empowerment of spiritual gifts working together collectively winning souls. Let us always be reminded that the greatest gift that remains permanent is love. *"And now abideth faith, hope charity, these three, but the greatest of these is charity" (I Corinthians 13:13).*

The Seven General Classifications of Ministries are found in Romans 12:6-9. The Ministry Gifts of Christ are given to fulfill an assigned ministry. Reading of Ephesians 4:7 and Ephesians 4:15 and 16 provide instruction on how these Ministry Gifts of Christ are to be used. In summary, the Ministry Gifts of Christ are Prophecy (in proportion to our faith), Service (use gift in serving), Teaching (use gift in teaching), Exhortation (use gift in exhorting—i.e., encouragement, personal work, and *soul winning*).

Many Specific Ministries are included in these General Classifications. Prophecy includes Apostles, Prophets, Evangelist, pastor and teacher, singer of psalms, the Gift of Prophecy, etc. Service includes deacons, deaconesses, ministry of helps, (including publishing work in the form of a newsletter, use of technology through the social media, janitors, clerical work, repair and maintenance work, etc. Teaching, includes elders, deacons, teachers of children, teachers of Bible classes, etc. Exhortation includes personal work, soul winning (Evangelism), Sunday services, and giving encouragement. Giving includes working of miracles, Gift of Faith, etc. Ruling includes apostles, prophets, pastors, elders, etc. Showing Mercy includes the elder ministry, ministry to the sick, helpers of the poor, care of orphans and widows and reaching out to visitors of the ministry, etc.

Now, no ministry is assumed. It is assigned by the Lord Jesus. We must not seek a place or refuse to fill the place God gives. These seven phases of Christ's endowment of ministries in the Body of Christ are found in varying combination according to the proportion of the grace and faith given to each ministry.

Two-Fold Ministry of the Church

Several Basic Ministries and Offices and Office in the Body of Christ are definitely named in *Ephesians 4:11-16* and *I Corinthians 12:27-31.*

In summary, *Ephesians 4:11-16 . . ." And he gave some, apostles some, prophets, some, evangelists, and some, pastors and teachers; For the perfecting of the saints, for the work of the ministry, for the edifying of the body of Christ:" I Corinthians 12:27-31* in summary, points to miracles, gifts of healings, helps, governments, and diversities of tongues.

Chapter 2

Ministering to the Masses in Preparation for the End-Time Harvest

"Do you not say, It is four months, until harvest time comes? Look! I tell you, raise your eyes and observe the fields and see how they are already white for harvesting." (John 4:35, Amplified)

"And he said unto them, Go ye into all the world, and preach the gospel to every creature." (Mark 16:15)

I. Who are the Masses?

II. Who Must Minister to the Masses?

III. Where Do We Minister to the Masses?

IV. When Do We Minister to the Masses?

V. How Do We Prepare to Minister to the Masses?

"Say not ye, there are yet four months, and then cometh harvest? Behold, I say unto you, lift up your eyes, and look on the fields; for they are white already to harvest." John 4:35

I. Who Are the Masses?

The Bible defines "masses" in *Mark 16:15,* *"And he said unto them, Go ye into all the world, and preach the gospel to every creature."* Masses is considered to mean every creature (person); the whole human race. Specifically in *Acts 1:8, "and ye shall be witnesses unto me both in Jerusalem, and in all Judea, an in Samaria, and unto the uttermost part of the earth." John 12:32 "And I, if I be lifted up from the earth [on the cross], will draw all men [Gentiles as well as Jews] to myself" (Amplified).*

The plan of God for *all* to be reached with the *gospel* (good news of Jesus Christ) is through the work or ministry of evangelism. The growth or increase of membership is the result of soul winning.

II. Who Must Minister to the Masses?

First, a People of Destiny, can be described as a *Chosen people.* It is important to read Jeremiah 1:4-10 and Ephesians 1:4. Secondly, a *Commissioned people, reading include Ephesians 4:11-12; Mark 16:15; and Acts 1:8.* Thirdly, an *Equipped people (John 17:18)* can be described (a) the *message* from Mark 16:15 and with *authority* from Luke 10:19 and Matthew 18:18.

Every member in any congregation should take on the responsibility to reach out to sinners and backsliders with love and the message of the good news.

Why must we minister? Like Jeremiah, we have a Divine Mandate. It breaks down like this:
> Go ye (Mark 16:15)
> Freely ye have received, freely give (Matthew 10:7-8)
> The harvest is ready to be brought in (John 4:35)
> It is our time (Matthew 20:6)
> It is means which God has chosen (I Corinthians 1:12)
> Luke 9:1-6 and Luke 10:1-3
> A pattern given; two by two (Acts 2)

III. Where Do We Minister to the Masses?

General: *"And about the eleventh hour he went out, and found others standing idle, and saith unto them, why stand ye here all the day idle? They say unto him, Because no man hath hired us. He saith unto them, Go ye also into the vineyard; and whatsoever is right, that shall ye receive." (Matthew 20:6-7)*

"Say not ye, There are yet four months, and then cometh harvest? Behold, I say unto you, Lift up your eyes, and look on the fields; for they are white already to harvest." (John 4: 35)

These two scriptures imply that the time is ripe and ready for soul winning or reap the harvest or people to the kingdom.

Specifically: *"Go ye therefore into the highways, and as many as ye shall find, bid to the marriage. So those servants went into the highways, and gathered together all as many as they found, both bad and good: and the wedding was furnished with guests." (Matthew 22:9-10)*

IV. When Do We Minister to the Masses?

No set time to do personal evangelism but corporately, a planned or set time should be scheduled as a ministry or church work. Now is the time and any today is an opportunity to win souls to the kingdom. There may be a set team that is recognized to sphere head the evangelistic ministry or outreach, but it should be emphasized that every believer can be involved in reaching out to sinners or backsliders. It is important to remember that our lives are on display for others to view. *Matthew 5:16 "Let your light so shine before men, that they may see your good works, and glorify your Father which is in heaven."* Finally, we are to minister *efficiently, effectively, consistently, and with urgency* in replying to reaching the lost at any cost.

V. How Do We Minister to the Masses?

First, it is important to recapture the vision and heed the mandate lost through the need to struggle with the cares of this life, the deceitfulness of riches, the pursuit of pleasure and the lust of other things.

In general, it is important to position the Church for evangelism or ministering to the masses: through training and persistent prayer, teaching the people *how* to evangelize and establishing a consistent follow-up program. Some churches call a follow-up program as closing the back door. Evangelism and a follow-up program will be explained more thoroughly in this book.

Second, methods of ministering to the masses can be placed within two categories, traditional and contemporary means.

I remember or classify traditional ways of ministering to large numbers or the masses, when revival services were scheduled periodically throughout the year. In my experience, the revivals would last for the minimum of a two week period. These services would include *prayer* on our knees to begin the service each night, following what was called *testimony service,* allowing the saints and opportunity to share the blessings from the Lord and overcoming victories, after which, *the preaching of the Word of God.* After the preached word, an *altar call* was extended for sinners and backsliders to come forth. The saints would gather around those that heeded the call or responded for deliverance. After the converts had asked God to forgive them of their sins collectively, for nearly an hour, they would *tarry* or repeatedly give exuberant praise unto God until the altar workers were convinced they were saved from their sins and had received the baptism of the Holy Ghost with the evidence of speaking in tongues. Of course, this was repeated the following nights until an individual could testify of God's gift of the Holy Ghost was evident and witnessed.

As one growing up in the church or particularly my denomination, I have witnessed another attempt to reach the masses: the conducting of Street services. The saints would choose certain corners, particularly where bars, pool halls, and taverns were located. They would bring instruments, sing, dance, and preach the Word of God. Altar Call would be extended, and sinners would respond in the open air services. I also experienced traveling in cars as a convoy. A line of cars would follow behind a car that had a megaphone. They would drive through neighborhoods slowly, compelling listeners to make Jesus their choice. The pastor would preach the Word of God with passion and a determination to reap a harvest of souls, traveling in the lead car. The message about Hell and damnation would get the attention of many listening while sitting on their porches. As I was recalling these times, I can remember my father playing his guitar, tambourines beating and the saints going forth in the Lord!

In preparation for revivals, I experienced another traditional phenomenal of the scheduling of Shut-ins. The saints would have at least three days of round-the-clock prayer, fasting or going without food and water, with church services included. Those who worked jobs and attended schools would attend the Shut-ins around their daily routine. Yes, even the children and teens were expected to participate as much as possible. I think back to a story that was told in order to draw a large crowd at one of the Street services. The pastor went to a street corner where the bar and pool hall was located across from each other. He stood at one of the corners and began to look up to the sky, not saying a word or responding to others that wanted to know what was he staring into the sky. Of course, others gathered around him and they begin to look up toward the sky. It was usually a busy corner, but traffic began to slow down when people were trying to see what was going on. What they didn't notice, the pastor was looking up but he also was aware of the crowd that had converged. When he was satisfied with the masses surrounding him, he opened his Bible and begin to preach the fiery message about Jesus Christ and repentance of sin. No one would walk away. Even if an individual didn't want to receive the gospel, that time, out of respect or fear about Hell, they would listen intently.

I think you would agree that these methods of reaching the masses are no longer practiced in what is called contemporary ways of doing things. The 21st-century churches now seems to rely on technological ways of reaching out to the masses.

The contemporary methods are promoted through the use of various technological uses of television ministries, internet interaction by connecting to Facebook, Twitter, LinkedIn, emailing, and texting. Let us not forget iPods, cell phones, smart phones, and the use of home phones.

It is my opinion that churches in general no longer schedule revival services as once was in the past. Of course, it is not widely known if any church, conduct two weeks as a common practice. It is common to hear of three days of consecutive services as a yearly event. Most ministries have shifted from revivals to conferences and workshops, etc. It appears that most do not schedule shut-ins either. Born and raised at a different time, and living in this present age, it is my opinion that some past practices had value and maybe should be revisited or implemented for this present day church. When you read in the Book of Acts at the early church, they traveled by foot, preached and testified where ever an opportunity presented itself and yet, many came to accept Christ. You can read Acts 2:41, where Peter preached and the Bible reports three thousand received Christ and was added to the church. Have you ever wondered like I, who counted to know the exact number and what was the follow up plan?

Numbers Do Count!

When you read Matthew 14: 13-21; Mark 6:30-44; Luke 9:10; and John 6:1-14, the examples of how Jesus drew the masses or multitude can be considered as a challenge, directive, and display how we can become effective in reaching large numbers to Christ. In each of these examples reveal that *someone* took the time to count and emphasize the totals. I think when citing these passages of scripture, it is evident that not enough focus is given to *what* Jesus did and *how* He achieved the results accomplished in each of those settings. As I took a closer look at each passage, it appeared that Jesus was teaching the church what need to be practiced so that the guarantee to winning souls or reaching the masses would be the result of every endeavor. First of all, Jesus became accessible to *where* the people would see Him. Secondly, He could "see" into their hearts the pain, struggle living victoriously, lack of happiness, not a real sense of direction and many needed physical healings. Thirdly, at the conclusion of His messages in every instance, He could identify with their hunger or need to be fed natural food. Never wanting to send any of them without knowing their stomachs were full. You will read that the Disciples, His handpicked and closest followers on more than one occasion, told Jesus to send the multitudes away because either they didn't have enough food or not enough money in the treasure to provide for such a large crowd. The Bible says that Jesus was testing them because He knew in each instance what was going to transpire; so that little would become much when placed in the Master's hand. Just a little faith can produce greater when allowing God to do on our behalf.

Fourthly, I examined more closely how Jesus attracted the men of that day with His message. Men were the heads of their households, providers to their families and set the standard for living for the wives and children regardless of region. In most of our churches and denominations, women have been the largest number for membership and involvement, with their children attending and participating. The males have either been absent from the home or not involved. It is my opinion that the "church" or body of believers in any local assembly must do more to reach the male gender. Fifthly, Jesus was able—for a period of time, while in His presence—bring structure to their day with Him. He would instruct the disciples in each case, to have the men sit in groups, as well with mothers and their children. This preparation prior to serving any meal, brought organization and fellowship as the people ate what was placed before them to be consumed. Well, what can we glean from this practice, as Jesus provided for the people? He fed them without charging them for what was served and the meal was filling. Fellowship was promoted, and there were fragments or food leftover. Finally, there were those who came one way, but after they were ministered to by Jesus, their physical bodies were made whole! It also teaches any ministry or local assembly, no matter the size of the congregation, if given to Jesus to bless efforts to reach souls, God will s-t-r-e-t-c-h and multiply so bring increase or reap a harvest! We have no excuse for not gaining a multitude in any assembly. It may not yield the four or five thousands at any setting, but *John 14:12* reads *"Most assuredly, I say to you, he who believes in Me, the works that I do he will do also; and greater works than these he will do, because I go to My Father."* John 12:32 reads, *"And I, if I am lifted up from the earth, will draw all men to unto me."*

As a member and serving in various leadership capacities, I understood the practice and reason for counting or giving accountability regarding services, events, activities, and meetings held at Victorious Believers Ministries. It became the duty of the usher board to count the attendance of individuals, regardless if it was a service, activity, event, or meeting. In addition to the attendance of all present, the count will include the vehicles on the parking lots of the church or facility being used offsite. Regardless, any gathering held by the church, even if it was offsite, this information was to be recorded. Bishop Pryor, as pastor of the church, would review and access the information gathered. Bishop Pryor wanted exactness, not exaggerations. It was important to him that the church would have creditable information. He could evaluate the growth, attendance, and participation during particular times of the year. The adage is "It is not enough just to have numbers, but numbers that count!" VBM had a responsibility to grow and work toward effectiveness to do what Jesus commanded, to *" draw all men unto me."*

As being the leader for evangelism at the local church and jurisdiction, my responsibility was to fulfill the vision for outreach. I directed the production of activities, such as conducting revival services, the disseminating of evangelism materials, prison services, and one on one witnessing as personal evangelism and corporate involvement. The local church combined their efforts with the VBM's Mission Department to feed and give away clothing and other items to those in need to receive, as the corporate body of Christ reached out into the communities of Saginaw, Michigan. We became the model for other churches within the jurisdiction to follow.

The bottom line, rather there should be merging of traditional and contemporary methods, the outcome is the most important thing to achieve, winning of souls to the kingdom! We have heard it said, "Time is running out." The Lord Jesus is making His return to this earth and every effort to reach the lost for Christ must be of urgency and priority! *"And I saw another angel fly in the midst of heaven, having the everlasting gospel to preach unto them that dwell on earth, and to every nation, and kindred, and tongue, and people." (Revelation 14:6)*

It is my hope that ministries will join me in prayer that God will put the need of revival will become a priority in churches throughout this world. The scheduling of revivals is the *call* of the senior pastor. *"But you be watchful in all things, endure afflictions, do the work of an evangelist, fulfill the work of the ministry" (II Timothy 4:5).*

When we read I Corinthians 12 and Ephesians 4, the spiritual gift of the evangelist is emphasized. There is a specific role to be accomplished by this *office of ministry,* which is labeled the Five Fold Ministry to be achieved if empowered to serve. The evangelist is the one who sets out to convert others to Christianity, by preaching the gospel or good news about Jesus Christ. It is my opinion that more time should be spent when assisting a convert in receiving the Spirit of Jesus Christ through the act of repentance. Maybe the traditional service of "tarrying" at the altar may no longer need to be experienced, but I believe what is required is more involvement in ministering to individuals who chose to accept Christ in their lives.

People in the Bible experienced the healing power of Jesus Christ. So people need to witness that God by His Son Jesus, through the power and authority of the Holy Spirit, is yet a healer of sicknesses and diseases. This will attract the attention of skeptics and unbelievers to draw the multitude or masses to Jesus Christ.

How to reach the masses, men of every birth,
for an answer Jesus gave the key:

"And I, if I be lifted up from the earth, Will draw all
men unto me."

Don't exalt the preacher, don't exalt the pew, preach the
Gospel simple, full and free;

Prove Him and you will find that promise is true, "I'll draw
all men unto Me."

Lift Him up,
Lift Him up, until He speaks from eternity:

"And I, if I be lifted up from the earth, will draw all
men unto Me."

—"Lift Him Up" by Johnson Oatman

Let's go fishing!

CHAPTER 3

Taking the First Step
Understanding the Basics: What is Sin?

Bible Verses Defining Sin:

John 20:31—Key to the Bible

"But these are written, that ye might believe that Jesus is the Christ, the Son of God; and that believing ye might have life through His name."

If the person believes that Jesus is the Son of God, congratulate him, and then ask, "Since believing, have you received God's gift of eternal life?" If he doesn't understand, it is evident that he has not received Christ. You can move to the next verse by saying, "Let me explain. There is a wall between every person and God. This wall is sin."

Romans 3:23—All Have Sinned

"For all have sinned, and come short of the glory of God." Continue with your prospect by saying, "This verse says everyone has sinned." That takes in the very best people so it would certainly mean you and me, wouldn't it? Yes, it would. (Once sin is admitted, move to the next verse.)

Romans 6:23—Penalty and Gift

"For the wages of sin is death; but the gift of God is eternal life through Jesus Christ our Lord."

After showing the person this verse, you can explain: This word death means separation from God forever in hell or, in other words, death of the soul. Just as a man receives wages for working, God pays wages to people for sinning. When we understand this and add, aren't you glad the verse doesn't end with death? Look at the second part again. God offers us the gift of eternal life. It's so valuable that you can't work for it or pay for it. That's why it has to be gift. Your part is to accept it.

John 3:16—Individual Importance

"For God so loved the world, that he gave his only begotten Son, that whosoever believeth in him, should not perish, but have everlasting life." Do you know how important you are to God? Then quote John 3:16, inserting that person's name. When you ask him who "whosoever" means he will probably answer, "Anybody." Agree and say it means you also.

We are taught that the Doctrine of Sin comes from a Greek word "hamartia" meaning sin. Hamartiology is the study of sin. Sin is missing the mark or falling short. *Romans 3:23 says, "For all have sinned and come short of the glory of God."*

Sin is the most comprehensive term for moral perversity or wickedness of mankind. The Bible says in, *Jeremiah 17:9 "The heart is deceitful above all things, and desperately wicked: who can know it."*

"But the things that come out of the mouth come from the heart, and these things defile a man. For out of the heart come evil thoughts, murder, adultery, sexual immorality, theft, false testimony, and slander. These are what defile a man . . ." (Matthew 15:18-20)

Romans 5, tells us from the disobedience of sin by Adam in Genesis 3, *life* has been possible through Jesus Christ being born, crucified, and resurrected.

"Wherefore, as by one man sin entered into the world, and death by sin; and so death passed upon all men, for that all have sinned: (For until the law sin was in the world: but sin is not imputed when there is no law. Nevertheless death reigned from Adam to Moses, even over them that had not sinned after the similitude of Adam's transgression, who is the figure of him that was to come. But not as the offence of one many be dead, much more the grace of God, and the gift by grace, which is by one man. Jesus Christ hath abounded unto many. And not as it was by one that sinned, so is the gift: for the judgment was by one to condemnation, but the free gift is of many offences unto justification. For if by one man's offence death reigned; by one much more they which receive abundance of grace and of the gift of righteousness shall reign in life by one, Jesus Christ.) For as by one man's disobedience many were made sinners, so by the obedience of one shall many be made righteous." (Romans 5:12-17,19)

Sin is listed as the works of the flesh when reading *Galatians 5:19-21: "Now the works of the flesh are evident, which are adultery, fornication, uncleanness, lewdness, idolatry, sorcery, hatred, contentions, jealousies, outbursts of wrath, selfish ambitions, dissensions, heresies, envy, murders, drunkenness, revelries, and the like, of which I tell you beforehand, just as I told you in time past, that those who practice such things will not inherit the kingdom of God."*

What Are Other Biblical Words for Sin?

1. Disobedience (Romans 5:19; Colossians 3:6; Hebrews 2:2)
2. Error (James 5:20; II Peter 2:18; 3:17)
3. Fault (Deuteronomy 25:2; I Peter 7:20)
4. Inequity (Acts 3:26; Romans 4:7; Titus 2:14)
5. Offense (Ecclesiastes 10:4; Romans 5:15-20; II Corinthians 11:7)

What Are Other Biblical Words for Sin?

6. Transgression (Romans 4:15; I John 3:4)
7. Ungodliness (Romans 1:18; II Timothy 2:16; Titus 2:12)
8. Unrighteousness (Romans 1:29; I John 1:9; 5:17)

Where Did Sin Originate?

The Bible teaches that sin originated in the heart of Lucifer, the angel who rebelled against God in heaven.

"Thou wast perfect in thy ways from the day that thou wast created, till inequity was found in thee. By the multitude of thy merchandise they have filled the midst of thee with violence, and thou hast sinned . . ." (Ezekiel 28:15, 16)

Sin began with Eve yielding to Satan's temptation in the Garden of Eden and when Adam was disobedient to God. *"And Adam was not deceived, but the woman being deceived was in the transgression"* (I Timothy 2:14).

Read Genesis 3. Sin actually entered when Adam, ate of the forbidden fruit.

"Wherefore, as by one man sin entered into the world, and death by sin; and so death passed upon all men, for that all have sinned . . .

For as by one man's disobedience many were made sinners, so by the obedience of one shall many be made righteous." (Romans 5:12, 19)

Are There Different Kinds of Sin?

9.   There are national sins (Proverbs 14:34)

10. There are personal sins (Joshua 7:20)

11. There are open sins (I Timothy 5:24)

12. There are secret sins (Psalms 90:8)

13. There are presumptuous sins (Psalms 19:13)

14. There are willful sins (Hebrews 10:26)

15. There is the sin of ignorance (Leviticus 4:2)

16. There is a sin of blasphemy, called the unpardonable sin (Matthew 12: 31,32)

17. There is a sin unto death (I John 5:16)

Chapter 4

Step 2: The Fish

Understanding the Basics:
What is a Sinner?

A Sinner is an individual that possesses a sin nature. The Bible says in Ephesians 2: 1-3, *"And you hath he quickened, who were dead in trespasses and sins; Wherein in time past ye walked according to the course of this world, according to the prince of the power of the air, the spirit that now worketh in the children of disobedience: Among whom also we all had our conversation in times past in the lusts of our flesh, fulfilling the desires of the flesh and of the mind; and were by nature the children of wrath, even as others."*

"Everyone who commits (practices) sin is guilty of lawlessness; for [that is what] sin is, lawlessness (the breaking), violating of God's law by transgression or neglect—being unrestrained and unregulated by His commands and His will." (I John 3:4, Amplified)

The Word of God is clear when is written, *"[But] he who commits sin [who practices evil doing] is of the devil [take his character from the evil one], for the devil has sinned (violated the divine law) from the beginning. The reason the Son of God was made manifest (visible) was to undo (destroy, loosen,* and dissolve) *the works the devil [has done]." (I John 3:8, Amplified)*

We, as Christians (Saints), must never forget that God doesn't hate sinners, but loves them. *John 3:16 reads, "For God so loved the world, that he gave his only begotten Son, that whosoever believeth in him should not perish, but have everlasting life."*

He hates the sin, but loves the sinner. *"Thou hast loved righteousness, and hated inequity; therefore God, even thy God, hath anointed thee with the oil of gladness above thy fellows." Hebrews 1:9* Also, Proverbs 6:16-19 reads *"These six things the Lord hates; indeed, seven are an abomination to Him: A proud look [the spirit that makes one overestimate himself and underestimate others], a lying tongue, and hands that shed innocent blood" (Psalms 120:2,3).*

A heart that manufactures wicked thoughts and plans, feet that are swift in running to evil, A false witness who breathes out lies [even under oath], and he who sows discord among his brethren."

What are some characteristics of a sinner? As we review from Romans 3:10-18, sinners can be identified as: Dealing with the Indifferent; Dealing with the Self-Righteous; Dealing with the Skeptics; Dealing with those who mouth is full of cursing and bitterness; Dealing with those who practice Destruction and misery in their own ways; Dealing with those who are Full of pride and deceitfulness and with those There is no fear of God before their eyes.

2. The Consequences of Sin and Unbelief

The scriptures listed give consequences to those that continue to practice sin daily and receive the consequence of their actions.

Isaiah 57:20, 21

"But the wicked are like the troubled sea, when it cannot rest, whose waters cast up mire and dirt. There is no peace, saith my God, to the wicked."

John 8:34, Amplified

Jesus answered them, I assure you, most solemnly I tell you, Whosoever commits and practices sin is the slave of sin."

Galatians 3:10

"For as many are of the works of the law are under the curse; for it is written, Cursed is every one that continueth not in all things which are written in the book of the law to do them."

John 3:36

He that believeth on the Son hath everlasting; and he that believeth not the Son shall not see life; but the wrath of God abideth on him."

John 3:18

"He that believeth on him is not condemned: but he that believeth not is condemned already, because he hath not believed in the name of the only begotten Son of God."

Romans 6:23

"For the wages of sin is death; but the gift of God is eternal life through Jesus Christ our Lord."

II Thessalonians 1:7-9

The Lord Jesus shall be revealed from heaven with his mighty angels in flaming fire taking vengeance on them that know not God, and that obey not the gospel of our Lord Jesus Christ; who shall be punished with everlasting destruction from the presence of the Lord, and from the glory of his power."

John 8:24

"Ye shall die in your sins: for if ye believe not that I am he, ye shall die in your sins."

CHAPTER 5

Step 3

Understanding the Basics: What Is Salvation?

Understanding the Basics About Salvation

Soteriology comes from the Greek word "soteria" meaning salvation. Soteriology is the study of salvation. It denotes deliverance, preservation, healing safety and soundness. Another definition says that salvation is the saving of a person from sin and its consequences, believed by Christians to be brought by faith in Jesus Christ.

Acts 2:38 says "Then Peter said unto them, Repent, and be baptized every one of you in the name of Jesus Christ for the remission of sins, and ye shall receive the gift of the Holy Ghost."

Romans 10:9-13 says "That if thou shalt confess with thy mouth the Lord Jesus, and shalt believe in thine heart God hath raised him from the dead, thou shalt be saved. For with the heart man beleieveth unto righteousness; and with the mouth confession is made unto salvation. For the scripture saith, Whosoever believeth on him shall not be ashamed. For there is no difference between the Jew and the

*Greek: for the same Lord over all is rich unto all that call upon him.
For whosoever shall call upon the name of the Lord shall be saved."*

Without the Resurrection, the death of Jesus Christ would be meaningless and powerless; it would have been equal only to the death of any human martyr. But through the Resurrection—the raising from the dead by the mighty power of God—the atoning work of the Son of God was perfect and complete. Because Christ rose from the dead, fulfilling His promise that He would do so, we have the assurance that when Christ returns in That Day for His own, we too shall rise from the dead to meet Him in the air!

All that we need for the forgiveness of our sins, for our justification, our salvation, our faith, and our hope, has been provided through Christ's death and resurrection. Not one of us deserves to be the recipient of such great love and sacrifice! Yet, through God's grace (His free, unmerited favor), it is ours for the taking, if we appropriate it through faith, and through repentance.

What Are the Scriptural Names for Salvation?
   A. Repentance
      —which means to have a change of mind in respect to man's relationship with God.

   Matthew 3:8, Amplified

   "Bring forth fruit that is consistent with repentance [let your lives prove your change of heart];"

   Mark 2:17

   "When Jesus heard it, he saith unto them, They that are whole have need of the physician, but they that are sick: I came not to call the righteous, but sinners to repentance."

Luke 3:3

> *"And he went into . . . preaching the baptism of repentance for the remission of sins."*

Acts 2:38

> *"Repent and be baptized."*

Acts 3:19

> *"Repent ye therefore, and be converted, that your sins may be blotted out."*

Acts 20:21

> *"Testifying both to the Jews, and also to the Greeks, repentance toward God, and faith toward our Lord Jesus Christ."*

II Corinthians 7:10, Amplified

> *For godly grief and the pain God is permitted to direct, produce a repentance that leads and deliverance from evil, and it never brings regret; but worldly grief (the hopeless sorrow that is characteristic of the pagan world) is deadly [bleeding and ending in death].*

Hebrews 6:1

> *Therefore leaving the principles of the doctrine of Christ, let us go on unto perfection; not laying again the foundation of repentance from dead works, and of faith toward God,"*

B. **Conversion**

—to turn about or around. It implies a turning from and a turning to.

Luke 22:32

> *"But I have prayed for thee, that thy faith fail not: and when thou art converted, strengthen thy brethren."*

James 5:19, 20

> *"Brethren, if any of you do err from the truth, and one convert him; Let him know, that he which converteth the sinner from the error of his way shall save a soul from death, and shall hide a multitude of sins."*

C. Regeneration
—new birth, re-creation; bring new life

Matthew 19:28

> *"And Jesus said unto them, Verily I say unto you, That ye which have followed me, in the regeneration when the Son of man shall sit in the throne of glory, ye also shall sit upon twelve thrones, judging the twelve tribes of Israel."*

II Corinthians 5:17

> *"Therefore if any man be in Christ, he is a new creature: old things are passed away; behold, all things are become new."*

Titus 3:5

> *"Not by works of righteousness which we have done, but according to his mercy he saved us, by the washing of regeneration, and renewing of the Holy Ghost;"*

D. Justification
—the act of pronouncing righteous; prove something to be right or reasonable

Romans 3:24, 28

> *"Being justified freely by his grace through the redemption that is in Christ Jesus:"*

> *"Therefore we conclude that a man is justified by faith without the deeds of the law."*

Romans 4:25

> *"Who was delivered for our offenses, and was raised again for our justification."*

Romans 5:1

> *"Therefore being justified by faith, we have peace with God through our Lord Jesus Christ:"*

E. **Redemption**

—a releasing for a ransom; save someone from sin or evil.

Romans 3:24

> *"Being justified freely by his grace through the redemption that is in Christ Jesus:"*

Galatians 3:13

> *"Christ hath redeemed us from the curse of the law, being made a curse for us: for it is written, Cursed is every one that hangeth on a tree."*

Romans 4:5, Amplified

> *"To purchase the freedom of (to ransom, to redeem, to atone for) those who were subject to the Law, that we might be adopted and have son-ship conferred upon us [and be recognized as God's sons].*

Hebrews 9:12

> *"Neither by the blood of goats and calves, but by his own blood be entered in once into the holy place, having ordained eternal redemption for us."*

F. **Deliverance**

—a release from bondage; the process of being set free

Luke 4:18

> *"The Spirit of the Lord is upon me, because he hath anointed me to preach the gospel to the poor, he hath*

sent me to heal the brokenhearted, to preach deliverance to the captives, and recovering of sight to the blind, to set at liberty them that are bruised,"

Galatians 1:4, Amplified

"Who gave (yielded) Himself up [to atone] for our sins [and to save and sanctify us], in order to rescue and deliver us from this present wicked age and world order, in accordance with the will and purpose and plan of our God and Father—"

Colossians 1:13

"Who hath delivered us from the power of darkness, and hath translated us into the kingdom of his dear Son."

Salvation or Repentance is manifested through:

1. Deep sorrow for sin and in self-humiliation and in self abhorrence.
2. In confession of sin and praying to God for mercy.
32. By the sinner turning away from his evil ways—from all his transgressions, his idols, his abominations, and his thoughts.
3. Turning to God to trust and serve Him.
4. Bringing forth fruit, or doing works, worthy of repentance.
5. Repentance is not merely abstinence from evil, but performance of good.

The Results of Salvation *they*:

1. No longer condemned. (*John 3:18*)
   "He that believeth on him is not condemned: but he that believeth not is condemned already, because he hath not believed in the name of the only begotten Son of God."

2. Have everlasting life. (John 3:36)

"He that believeth on the Son hath everlasting life: and he that believeth not the Son shall not see life; but the wrath of God abideth on him."

3. Become a new creature. (*II Corinthians 5:17*)
"*Therefore if any man be in Christ, he is a new creature: old things are passed away; behold, all things become new.*"

4. Become the children of God. (*Romans 8:16*)
"*The Spirit itself beareth witness with our spirit, that we are the children of God:*"

5. Become the heirs of God. *(Romans 8:17)*
"*And if children, then heirs; heirs of God, and joint-heirs with Christ; if so be that we suffer with him, that we may be also gathered together.*"

6. Have the peace of God, neither be afraid. *(John 14:27, Amplified)*
"*Peace I leave with you; My [own] peace I now give and bequeath to you. Not as the world gives do I give to you. Do not let your hearts be troubled, neither let them be afraid. [Stop allowing yourselves to be agitated and disturbed; and do not permit yourselves to be fearful and intimidated and cowardly and unsettled.]*"

7. They have the Spirit of God dwell within. (*Romans 8:9*)
"*But ye are not in the flesh; but in the Spirit, if so be that the Spirit of God dwell in you. Now if any man have not the Spirit of Christ, he is none of his.*"

8. Have their names written in the book of life. *(Philippians 4:3, Amplified)*
"*And I exhort you too, [my] genuine yokefellow, help these [two women to keep on cooperating], for they have toiled along with me in [the spreading of] the good news (the Gospel), as have Clement and the rest of my fellow workers whose names are in the Book of Life.*"

In conclusion regarding the lesson on Salvation, there are points to be remembered. We have an Assurance of Salvation that has been already purchased by the price of the precious Blood of Christ and eternal life is offered as a gift to all who believe.

"For by grace are ye saved through faith; and that not of yourselves; it is the gift of God: Not of works, lest any man should boast." (Ephesians 2:8, 9)

We will possess a compassionate love of the brethren, sinners and backsliders.

"We know that we have passed from death unto life, because we love the brethren. He that loveth not his brother abideth in death." (I John 3:14)

The love of God shed abroad in the heart by the Holy Spirit.

"And hope maketh not ashamed; because the love of God is shed abroad in our hearts by the Holy Ghost which is given unto us." (Romans 5:5)

Understanding the Basics for Salvation

Promise of Assurance results in:

1. Evidence of Salvation.
2. Love of the brethren [I John 3:14].
3. The witness of the Spirit [I John 5:10; Romans 8:16]
4. The leading of the Spirit [Romans 8:14].
5. The love of God shed abroad in the heart by the Holy Spirit [Romans 5:5; Galatians 5:22].

6. The fruit of the Spirit Galatians 5:22, 23].
7. Keeping the commandments of Christ
   [I John 2:3-6; 3:23, 24].
8. Doing righteousness [I John 3:10].
9. Willingness to confess Christ publicly [Romans 10:9, 10; Matthew 10:32, 33; I John 4:2].
10. Spiritual understanding [I John 2:20, 27; 5:20; I Corinthians 2:12-15].

CHAPTER 6

Step 4: The Bait

What Is the Gospel?

Before anyone can accurately communicate the gospel, it is necessary to clearly understand what it means. Here is a simple acronym to help understand its meaning and purpose from scriptures.

GOSPEL

G

"Go ye therefore, and teach all nations, baptizing them in the name of the Father, and of the Son, and the Holy Ghost: Teaching them to observe all things whatsoever I have commanded you: and, lo, I am with you always, even unto the end of the world. Amen." (Matthew 28:19, 20)

"... Go ye into all the world, and preach the gospel to every creature." (Mark 16:15)

O

"Our Saviour Jesus Christ, who hath abolished death, and hath brought life and immorality to light through the gospel." *(II Timothy 1:10)*

"Our liberty which we have in Christ Jesus." *(Galatians 2:4)*

"... O Lord, my strength, and my redeemer." (*Psalms 19:14*)

S

"*Stand fast therefore in the liberty wherewith Christ hath made us free, and be not entangled again with the yoke of bondage.*" (Galatians 5:1, 13)

"*So Christ was once offered to bear the sins of many; and unto them that look for him shall he appear the second time without sin unto salvation.*" *(Hebrews 9:28)*

"Shew forth the praises of Him who hath called you out of darkness into His marvelous light." (*I Peter 2:9*)

P

"*Whom God hath set forth to be a propitiation through faith in his blood, to declare his righteousness for the remission of sins that are past, through the forbearance of God;*" (Romans 3:25)

"*For all the promises of God in him are yea, and in him Amen, unto the glory of God by us.*" (*I Corinthians 1:20*)

"Whereby are given unto us exceeding great and precious promises; that by these ye might be partakers of the divine nature, having escaped the corruption that is in the world through lust." *(II Peter 1:4)*

E

"*... but the gift of God is eternal life through Jesus Christ our Lord.*" *(Romans 6:23)*

"*And this is the promise that he hath promised us, even eternal life.*" *(1 John 2:25)*

"But the Lord is faithful, who will establish you and guard you from the evil one. And we have confidence in the Lord concerning you, both that you will do and will do the things we command you." (II Thessalonians 3:3)

"Every good gift and every perfect gift is from above, and comes down from the Father of lights, with whom there is no variation or shadow of turning." (James 1:17)

L

*"Love never fails . . ." (*I Corinthians 13:8)

"Love has been perfected among us in this: that we may have boldness in the day of judgment; because as He is, so are we in this world." (I John 4:17)

God has good news for us! It is called the gospel—which means good news, good tidings, or good message. It can be summed up when we read and believe *John 3:16: "For God so loved the world, that He gave His only begotten Son, that whosoever believeth in Him should not perish, but have everlasting."*

Our faith, from this one verse can be a foundation for our entire belief. We can understand that it is the gospel [the good news] from God, through His Son, Jesus Christ by the power of the Holy Ghost to receive love.

The gospel brings in great abundance of joy, and light, and life, and hope, and blessing, and peace, and immortality. How to receive this gospel? First, we hear it, and repent from our sins and believe the gospel to live it!

"Behold, I bring you good tidings of great joy, which shall be to all people. For unto you is born this day in the city of David a Saviour, which is Christ the Lord." (Luke 2:10, 11)

"We were allowed of God to be put in trust with the gospel." (I Thessalonians 2:4)

Reference Scriptures: Why did Jesus Christ come to earth?

This list of statements have been compiled with the scriptures from the New Testament regarding what we are to do with the Gospel or what has happened for us because of the Gospel. Please take the time to read; study and make practice.

- Proclaim the Gospel

    [Paul is the preacher] *"And straightway he preached Christ in the synagogues, that he is the Son of God." (Acts 9:20)*

    "And when they were at Salamis, they preached the word of God in the synagogues of the Jews: and they had also John to their minister." (Acts 13:5)

    "But ye are a chosen generation, a royal priesthood, an holy nation, a peculiar people; that ye should show forth the praises of him who hath called you out of darkness into his marvelous light:" (I Peter 2:9)

- Preach the Gospel

    "And there they preached the gospel." (Acts 14:7)

"So, as much as in me is, I am ready to preach the gospel to you that are at Rome also." (Romans 1:15)

"For we stretch not ourselves beyond our measure, as though we reached not unto you; for we are come as far as to you also in preaching the gospel of Christ: Not boasting of things without our measure, that is, of other men's labours; but having hope, when your faith is increased, that we shall be enlarged by you according to our rule abundantly. To preach the gospel in the regions beyond you, and not to boast in another man's line of things make ready to our hand." (Acts 10:14-16)

- Believe the Gospel

  "And saying, The time is fulfilled, and the kingdom of God is at hand: repent ye, and believe the gospel." (Mark 1:15)

  "And when there had been much disputing, Peter rose up, and said unto them, Men and brethren, ye know how that a good while ago God made choice among us, that the Gentiles by my mouth should hear the word of the gospel, and believe." (Acts 15:7)

- Lose your life for the Gospel

  "For whosoever will save his life shall lose it; but whosoever shall lose his life for my sake and the gospel's, the same shall save it." (Mark 8:35)

- Some people are especially set apart for the Gospel

  "I Paul, a servant of Jesus Christ, called to be an apostle, separated unto the gospel of God," (Romans 1:1)

- Don't be ashamed of the Gospel

  "For I am not ashamed of the gospel of Christ: for it is the power of God unto salvation to everyone that believeth; to the Jew first, and also to the Greek." (Romans 1:16)

- You are parents and children of others because of the Gospel

"For though ye have ten thousand instructors in Christ, yet ye not many fathers: for in Christ Jesus I have begotten you through the gospel." (I Corinthians 4:15)

- Some people will earn and receive their living from the Gospel

  "Even so hath the Lord ordained that they which preach the gospel; should live of the gospel." (I Corinthians 9:14)

- Do all things for the sake of the Gospel

  "And this I do for the gospel's sake, that I might be partaker thereof with you." (I Corinthians 9:23)

- You are fellow partakers in the Gospel

  "And this I do for the gospel's sake, that I might be partaker thereof with you." (I Corinthians 9:23)

- Make known the Gospel

  "Moreover brethren, I declare unto you the gospel when I preached unto you, which also ye have received, and wherein ye stand;" (I Corinthians 15:1)

- Stand in the Gospel

  "Moreover brethren, I declare unto you the gospel when I preached unto you, which also ye have received, and wherein ye stand;" (I Corinthians 15:1)

- You might achieve fame in the Gospel (not for yourself, but your service and character for the cause of Christ

  "And we have sent with him the brother, whose praise is in the gospel throughout all the churches;" (II Corinthians 8:18)

- Do not abandon the Gospel for another gospel

"I marvel that ye are so soon removed from him that called you into the grace of Christ unto another gospel; Which is not another; but there be some that trouble you, and would pervert the gospel of Christ." (Galatians 1:6, 7)

- The truth of the Gospel remains with you

"To whom we gave place by subjection, no, not for an hour; that the truth of the gospel might continue with you." (Galatians 2:5)

- You have been entrusted with the Gospel

"But contrariwise, when they saw that the gospel of the un-circumcision was committed me, as the gospel of the circumcision was unto Peter;" (Galatians 2:7)

- Be straightforward about the truth of the Gospel

"But when I saw that they walked not uprightly according to the truth of the gospel, I said unto Peter before them all, if thou, being a Jew, lives after the manner of Gentiles, and not as do the Jews, why compelled from thou Gentiles to live as do the Jews?" (Galatians 2:14)

- You are a fellow partaker of the promise of Christ Jesus through the Gospel

"That the Gentiles should be fellow heirs, and of the same body, and partakers of his promise in Christ by the gospel:" (Ephesians 3:6)

- Participate in the Gospel

"For your fellowship in the gospel from the first day until now;" (Philippians 1:5)

Develop Your Skills as a Fisher of Men

"Follow me and I will make you fishers of men." Matthew 4:19

- One becomes a fisherman by fishing, just begin to do it and let the method unfold itself.

- Success in fishing is conditioned upon skill as well as the right kind of equipment.

- Skill is the outcome of experience.

- A fisherman must keep out of sight. Hide behind the cross.: *And I; if I be lifted up . . . will draw . . ." John 12:32*

- He will use tact—one must not scare the fish. An experienced fisherman will not *land* or *skin* the fish.

- Be guided by the Holy Spirit so that the fisherman will do and say the right thing.

- Attempt to have your conduct reflect the love of Christ.

- Keep your "pole or net" used for fishing refreshed [Pray and Study the Word of God] daily.

Why Did Jesus Die and was Resurrect?

Jesus Christ died because of His great, incapable-to-be-fully-understood love for us. He does not want anyone to perish but to repent and be forgiven, and have eternal life. He cannot save or deliver us while we are still in our sins. There is nothing at all anyone can do on his own to obtain, or in any way merit or qualify for being good enough on their own without salvation.

God has decreed that without the shedding of blood there is no remission or forgiveness of sins [Hebrews 9:22), but only the shedding of the blood of God's only Son, Jesus Christ, the Sinless One, could be that which would appease or satisfy God (or be the propitiation) for our sins. The cross and the suffering of Jesus Christ for us gives God's estimate of sin, and the punishment He thinks is deserved by sinful man since the disobedience by Adam from the beginning of time. If there were any other way to make salvation available to us, Christ would not have suffered, bled, and died on our behalf.

Without the Resurrection, the death of Jesus Christ would be meaningless and powerless; it would have been equal only to the death of any human martyr. But through the Resurrection—the raising from the dead by the mighty power of God was perfect and complete. Because Christ rose from the dead, fulfilling His promise that He would do so—we have the assurance that when Christ returns in *That Day* for His own, we too shall rise from the dead to meet Him in the air!

All that we need for the forgiveness of our sins, for our justification, our salvation, our faith, and our hope, has been provided through Christ's death and resurrection. Not a one of us deserves to be the recipient of such great love and sacrifice! Yet, through God's grace (His free, unmerited favor), it is ours for the taking, if we appropriate it through faith, and through repentance.

CHAPTER 7

What Is Evangelism?

Evangelism for the Purpose of Godliness by the Late Bishop Marvin C. Pryor

Evangelism is a broad subject, and there are things about it that I want to share and explain in this chapter. Godliness requires that we discipline ourselves in the practice of evangelism.

Building Block #1: Awareness

What Is Evangelism?

Evangelism is discussed much, but explained little in our churches today. *"To evangelize"* literally means to gossip the good news of our deliverance from sin by Jesus Christ the Saviour with unbelievers, as stated in *Acts 8:4: "Therefore they that were scattered abroad went every where preaching the word."* The reason why pastors are often unexcited, not involved and unsuccessful in evangelism is because we concentrate on telling the "good news" to saints rather than sinners. Our congregations need to be more aware of, and involved with the unbelieving world around them. We have not been in the practice of thinking gossip to be positive, but always referred negatively. The true definition for the word gossip is to talk about another person in a casual conversation to another.

In order to build this awareness, evangelism should have top priority in all membership, discipleship, and department/ auxiliary training objectives and written materials. When planning special events, we should always ask how this activity relates to the unbeliever. When presenting a fiscal budget, home and foreign missions must be a priority item. If we are not budgeting to purchase or print outreach materials, if we are not meeting people's needs and promoting Christ outside of the church; if we are not pushing for growth wherever possible, our leadership will not be aware of evangelism's importance to the overall church program. There is no growing without setting goals in giving and going.

Every deacon board and missionary circle should walk with Jesus through His methodology on building awareness of evangelism's priority into leadership. Jesus' "highways and byways" philosophy is reflected in His sending out disciples two by two as in *Mark 6:7, "And he called unto him the twelve, and begin to send them forth by two and two; and gave them power over unclean spirits;"* in lovingly confronting publicans, *Matthew 11:19, "The Son of man came eating and drinking, and they say, Behold a man gluttonous, and a winebibber, a friend of publicans and sinners. But wisdom is justified of her children.";* in speaking to large and small crowds, *Luke 9:13, "But he said unto them, Give ye them to eat. And they said, We have no more but five loaves and two fishes; except we should go and buy meat for all this people;"* and in sharing who He was one-on-one, even when it was to a woman in *John 4:7, 28, 29 and 39 "There cometh a woman of Samaria to draw water: Jesus saith unto her, Give me to drink . . . The woman then left her waterpot, and went her way into the city, and saith unto the men, Come see a man, which told me all things that ever I did: is not this the Christ? And many of the Samaritans of that city believed on him, for the saying of the woman, which testified, He told me all that I ever did."*

Before He ascended, Jesus gave his first leadership team a prioritized Holy Spirit territory-taking strategy: *"But ye shall receive power, after that the Holy Ghost is come upon you: and ye shall be witnesses unto me both in Jerusalem, and in all Judea, and in Samaria, and unto the uttermost part of the earth" (Acts 1:8).*

Building Block #2: Announcement

Besides building an awareness of evangelism into our overall church program and leadership, we need to challenge our cities by "announcing" the good news. To "proclaim" the Gospel literally means to thoroughly announce Jesus to unbelievers as in many living and labor situations as possible as in *Luke 9:60 "Jesus said unto him, Let the dead bury their dead: but go thou and preach the kingdom of God."*

Pulpit preaching does not change cities. Committed people change cities, and they do it by announcing Jesus and inviting others to know Him in a clear and positive way! Friendly friends make more friends. Preachers, in turn, help turn friends into faithful disciples.

This is why we must evaluate who we are announcing the Gospel to; why they are or are not open to our call, and how effectively Christ is being both communicated and received.

Within the church, our normal "proclamation days" center around holidays, revivals, concerts, missions, conventions, and special occasions or guest speakers. These church-based efforts are fine, but represent only a small part of an evangelistic strategy. Many of these speakers and short campaigns are tailored to our church members' likes and dislikes, and not to those of the unbeliever.

Now, as you fast and pray, believe God to broaden your announcement strategy. Identify how effectively you are in reaching children, high school and college students, factory workers, special-interest groups. socioeconomic, and social-issues groups, government officials, sports' teams, community and media VIPs, and the general populous that live around your church,

Take time to write down these and other groups. Examine your annual calendar and fiscal budget allocations. Most of us talk about these people, but do not plan, fundraiser or pay to preach the Gospel, or have the Gospel preached to them. Most of them do not know we exist. We need to identify them and see if and how we are reaching them.

All of us get excited when we feel we know where God is directing us. After identifying our community and those groups that God's Spirit is prompting us to concentrate on, then we can begin to schedule and produce children and adult visitation teams, print/radio/television campaigns, direct-mail promotions for seasonal and special events, community service evangelistic involvement in city fairs, Fourth of July festivals, mayors' prayer breakfasts, anti-drug/alcohol/pornography/crime concerns, phone campaigns, and city clean up. Our commitment to our commands respect for Christ. Earning the right to be heard is the biggest obstacle to effective evangelism. Building relationships with unbelievers in every possible avenue of respectable community life demonstrates your loving concern for people.

Building Block #3: Acceptance

As motivated, aware leadership and laity continuously and thoroughly announce Christ, many begin to "accept" Him as the Christ, dektos:

"And he said, Verily I say unto you, No prophet is accepted in his own country" (Luke 4:24) The key to evaluating and maintaining our evangelism efforts centers on how we view "acceptance."

Evaluating our outreach effectiveness can be deduced from how it was reported in the New Testament through signs and wonders, *John 2:11, "This beginning of miracles did Jesus in Cana of Galilee, and manifested forth his glory; and his disciples believed on him."* Numbers counted, *Acts 2:41, "Then they that gladly received his word were baptized: and the same day there were added unto them about three thousand souls";* church in *Acts 2:47, "Praising God, and having favour with all the people. And the Lord added to the church daily such as should be saved."*

Evangelistic decisions or initial acceptance does not constitute effectiveness. True "acceptance" of the Gospel must turn into affirmation of what Christ has done and is doing in someone's life. *"And all that believed were together, and had all things common: And sold their possessions and goods, and parted them to all men, as every man had need, in the temple, and breaking bread from house to house, did eat their meat with gladness and singleness of heart"* *(Acts 2:44-46).*

Programming for acceptance then deals initially with prayer and fasting. *"Is not this the fast that I have chosen? To loose the bands of wickedness, to undo the heavy burdens, and to let the oppressed go free, and that ye break every yoke? Is it not to deal thy bread to the hungry, and that thou bring the poor that are "cast out to thy house? when thou seest the naked, that thou cover him; and that thou hide not thyself from thine own flesh? Then shall thy light break forth as the morning, and thine health shall spring forth speedily: and thy righteousness shall shall go before thee; the glory of the Lord shall be thy reward"* (Isaiah 58:6-8).

In your daily prayer time and weekly prayer groups, home fellowship meetings, or intercessors' prayer chains, have believers pray for open eyes, hearts, and minds of unbelievers in *Matthew 9:30, "And their eyes were opened; and Jesus straitly charged them, saying, See that no man know it."*

Secondly, secure a good follow-up system to work for everyone who accepts Christ. Include a call, a letter, a visit and a dinner/ event/service invitation to everyone expressing interest, accepting Christ, or coming to church. Use trained couples from your deacons, or leadership group to be assigned, one couple at a time, to the new converts. There are a number of 6-, 8-, 10-, 15-step discipleship programs which can be taught one-on-one in the home. An ongoing discipleship class or new believers must be taught continually, regardless of the number meeting.

When someone accepts Christ, be ready to accept them. The reason more churches hire high-powered evangelists is because they want numbers, but they are not ready for disciples. The average disciple or church-placed rate is two to five percent, one year after a mass campaign, unless acceptance is both initially secured and continually maintained.

As we approach the mid-point of the Decade of Harvest, let us be aware, let us identify and plan to announce the Gospel, and let us be ready to accept those who do accept Jesus as Savior!"

Ways and Means as **Evangelistic Opportunities**

1. "Adopt" a family from within the community that assistance will be provided. The object is to help families become self-sufficient, and not "code dependent."
2. Become a Big Sister or Big Brother through the means of social programs in your community.
3. Become a Pen Pal to someone in prison or armed forces. Sharing the Word of God, prayer and encouragement.
4. Begin a Prayer chain with believers using phone services (Conference Calls).
5. Contact a Senior Citizen on a regular basis to encourage and serve as needed.
6. Collect clothing, food, furniture and toys at Christmas and for emergencies throughout your community.
7. Conduct outdoor services regularly in your community.
8. "Drive by" Prayer vigils throughout neighborhoods where crime and violence is on the increase. If possible, use church van for identification, announcing to the neighborhoods that the church is on a "prayer watch" for God's divine intervention.
9. Email individuals with a prayer and word of encouragement.

10. Form teams from within the local church that will walk through the neighborhood where they live to pray, pass tracts and witness.

11. Finance a ministry that is helping adults and children through missions.

12. Join a team that will provide ministry service in the jails and/or prisons in your city.

13. Join a team or through the missions' department, provide meals to families or individuals during Thanksgiving and/or Christmas holidays.

14. Join a team that will devote a set time to pray for the president, congress, mayor, city officials, and police departments regularly.

15. Form a team that will select school districts within the communities to pray for daily. When possible, pray at those schools within the communities. If there are staff, including teachers and students that are known, call out their names specifically.

16. Leave a tip for a waiter or waitress with a tract.

17. Periodically collect items from members within the congregation to give out to those in need within the community.

18. Reach out to backsliders by the means of prayer, send a card, and provide a need.

19. Serve as a volunteer at a Men's or Women's shelter in your community.

20. When you hear and see television and radio stories of situations reporting devastation, extend a helping hand.

21. Visit convalescent homes and nurseries throughout the community to provide church services and personal needs.

22. Volunteer to serve through foreign missions opportunities.

23. Reach out to churches in your community to combine forces to combat the life of deprivation placed upon individuals.
24. Witness opportunities through the use of tracts and other printed materials that can be handed out and mailed.
25. SWAT (Soul Winning Across Town) activities founded and practiced by Bishop Bob Jackson from Los Angeles, California.

CHAPTER 8

Witnessing, the Work of Evangelism

Is Witnessing Expected of Every Christian?

Yes, every believer has their own particular role to perform, when it comes to winning souls. The Bible likens the body of believers to the physical body, with each member (no matter how seemingly small and insignificant) being essential to the smooth working of the whole body. Each person has his own part to play: each has his own spiritual gift. Read Ephesians 4:11-16 and II Corinthians 12.

The responsibility of getting out the gospel was never intended to rest solely upon preachers, teachers, evangelists, and missionaries. Every one of us is expected to play a very real part in the cause of Christ. Laymen, or those in the pews, in their daily walk and work, will be in places each day where they can witness on a more equal, and meaningful basis than can, perhaps, the clergy that preaches from the pulpit. Matter fact, *John 14:12* says, *"Verily, verily, I say unto you, He that believeth on me, the works, that I do shall he do also; and greater works than these shall he do; because I go unto my Father."* The duties of all Christians never cease, for we are to be full time Christians. Every contact we have with others, every attitude, every conversation, every letter, every deed, every greeting says something to others. Since the use technology, email messages, Facebook, LinkedIn, or Twitter, etc., are means to reach out to spread the *good news* of the Gospel.

I remember, as a child, going fishing with my father and catching fish. Sometimes I would have to cast the smaller or baby fish back in the lake because they were too small to be skinned. Of course, this was disappointing to me, after my efforts to bait the hook with a worm and my efforts weren't rewarded by my catch.

Fishing for Souls is different, because Jesus said in *Mark 10:13-15, "And they brought young children to him, that he should them; and his disciples rebuked those that brought them. But when Jesus saw it, he was much displeased, and he said unto them, Suffer the little children to come unto me, and forbid them not; for of such is the kingdom of God. Verily I say unto you, Whosoever shall not receive the kingdom of God as a little child, he shall not enter therein."*

We may be the only example of Christianity that some have ever seen. We, as believers, are all here to advance the cause of Jesus Christ, and, as such, are all "missionaries" wherever He leads us—even if it is no farther than the four walls of a sickroom. Our "mission field" is all the unsaved people with whom we come in contact. Each one of them is looking for something which is unfulfilled in his life. May we give him bread and not a stone, and may we love each to Christ.

What Is Witnessing?

Witnesses—Jesus told them in *Acts 1:8, "But ye shall receive power, after that the Holy Ghost is come upon you: and ye shall be witnesses unto me both in Jerusalem, and in all Judea, and in Samaria, and unto the uttermost part of the earth."*

To define a witness, let's think about it in non-religious terms. A witness is simply someone who *"has personal knowledge of something"* and *"testifies and gives evidence to others of a fact or event."* Witnessing is just telling other people what you've seen, heard, and experienced.

The apostle John said in *John 1:7, "The same came for a witness, to bear witness of the Light; that all men through him might believe."* What a simple statement of what a witness for God is to do—*"testify of the light,"* and why we witness—*"so others might believe."* We also see this in the story about the Samaritan woman at the well—*"many of the Samaritans believed in Jesus because of the woman who testified"* in John 4:39.

Others can and will believe in Jesus Christ because of our testimony and what we say and do! What an incredible responsibility, privilege, and opportunity—to be carriers of the message of eternal life so that others will believe through us.

When we witness to others about Jesus Christ, He is actually sending Himself out through you and me. Just telling others about eternal life and what we have experienced is something sacred and imperishable.

Witnessing is like the *pole* or *net* from which the *Gospel, as the bait,* is connected in order to catch a soul or souls. You witness when you tell others about something that affected you very personally. The disciples were just telling people what they Jesus do, what they heard Him teach, and what they were personally experiencing. Your experience, what happened to you directly is important to the witness of Jesus Christ in your own life. I call it *"One on one"* or *Personal evangelism* is yet needed throughout the Body of Christ.

A witness should possess *Passion, Knowledge,* and *Training* to be effective.

A. Passion

A passion or intense enthusiasm to know Jesus Christ and to make Him known wherever and whenever the opportunity present itself.

Luke 14:23
"And the lord said unto the servant, Go out unto the highways and hedges, and compel them to come in, that my house may be filled."

Acts 4:20
"For we cannot but speak the things which we have seen and heard."

B. Knowledge

Peter's last words in his final letter tells us to *"grow in the grace and knowledge of our Lord and Savior Jesus Christ"* (II Peter 3:18). There are four significant areas of knowledge—things that a witness should know:

1. God's Heart and Purpose

Luke 19:10
"For the Son of Man has come to seek and to save that which was lost."

John 3:16

For God so loved the world, that He gave His only begotten Son, that whosoever believes in Him shall not perish, but have eternal life."

II Corinthians 5:21

"He made Him who knew no sin to be sin on our behalf, so that we might become the righteousness of God in Him"

I Timothy 2:4, 5

"Who will have all men to be saved, and to come unto the knowledge of the truth; For there is one God, and one mediator between God and men, the man Christ Jesus;"

II Peter 3:9

"The Lord is not slack concerning his promise, as some men count slackness; but is longsuffering to us-ward, not willing that any should perish, but that all should come to repentance."

2. The Believer's Role and Purpose

II Corinthians 5:18-20

"And all things are of God, who hath reconciled us to himself by Jesus Christ, and hath given to us the ministry of reconciliation; To wit, that God was in Christ, reconciling the world unto himself, not imputing their trespasses unto them; and hath committed unto us the word of reconciliation. Now then we are ambassadors for Christ, as though God did beseech you by us: we pray you in Christ's stead, be ye reconciled to God."

Philippians 3:8

"Yea doubtless, and I count all things but loss for the excellency of the knowledge of Christ Jesus my Lord: for whom I have suffered the loss of all things, and do count them but dung, that I may win Christ,"

I Timothy 2:5

"For there is one God; and one mediator between God and men, the man Christ Jesus;"

3. The Status of Those in Sin and Without Christ

Isaiah 59:2

"But your iniquities have separated between you and your God, and your sins have hid his face from you, that he will not hear."

Romans 3:23

"For all have sinned, and come short of the glory of God;"

Romans 6:23a

"For the wages of sin is death;"

I John 5:12b

"... and he that hath not the Son of God hath not life."

4. The Truth about Salvation

John 14:6

"Jesus saith unto him, I am the way, the truth, and the life: no man cometh unto the Father, but by me."

Acts 4:12

"Neither is there salvation in any other: for there is none other name under the heaven given among men, whereby we must be saved."

Romans 6:23b

"Whoever will call upon the name of the Lord will be saved."

Romans 10:13

"For whosoever shall call upon the name of the Lord shall be saved."

I John 5:11, 12a

"And this is the record; that God hath given to us eternal life, and this life is in his Son."

C. Training

As Christians, we have been very critical of religions that don't carry the right message, but have the right method for one on one witnessing. They knock on our doors and bring printed materials regarding what they believe; which is contrary to the teachings of the Bible.

These individuals are instructed and trained before being sent out to convert others to their doctrine. They anticipate problems, rejections, and discussions and have been trained how to respond. How much more should we be instructed and trained *how* to present ourselves in order to be effective?

While the emphasis of a witness is on *being*, there is still the essence and importance of *doing*. Paul told Timothy, in *II Timothy*

2:2, *"And the things that thou hast heard of me among many witnesses, the same commit thou to faithful men, who shall be able to teach others also."*

Study the Bible and the Evangelism Lessons

Proverbs 16:3, Amplified

"Roll your works upon the Lord [commit and trust them wholly to Him;

He will cause your thoughts to become agreeable to His will, and] so shall your plans be established and succeed."

Proverbs 22:6, Amplified

"Train up a child in the way he should go [and in keeping with his individual gift or bent], and when he is old he will not depart from it."

I Corinthians 14:40

"Let all things be done decently and in order."

II Timothy 2:15

"Study to show thyself approved unto God, a workman that needeth not to be ashamed, rightly dividing the word of truth."

II Timothy 3:15 Amplified

"And how from your childhood you have had a knowledge of and been acquainted with the Writings, which are able to instruct you and give you the understanding for salvation which comes through faith in Christ Jesus [through the learning of the entire human personality on God in Christ Jesus in absolute trust and confidence in His power, wisdom, and goodness]."

Colossians 4:6, Amplified

"Let your speech at all times be gracious (pleasant and winsome), seasoned [as it were] with salt, [so that you may never be at a loss] to know how you ought to answer anyone [who puts a question to you]."

Chapter 8

Witnessing, the Work of Evangelism

Is witnessing expected of every Christian?
Yes, every believer has their own particular role to perform, when it comes to winning souls. The Bible likens the body of believers to the physical body, with each member (no matter how seemingly small and insignificant) being essential to the smooth working of the whole body. Each person has his own part to play: each has his own spiritual gift. [Read Ephesians 4:11-16 and II Corinthians 12]

The responsibility of getting out the gospel was never intended to rest solely upon preachers, teachers, evangelists, and missionaries. Every one of us is expected to play a very real part in the cause of Christ. Laymen, or those in the pews, in their daily walk and work, will be in places each day where they can witness on a more equal, and meaningful basis than can, perhaps, the clergy that preaches from the pulpit. Matter fact, *John 14:12 "Verily, verily, I say unto you, He that believeth on me, the works, that I do shall he do also; and greater works than these shall he do; because I go unto my Father."* The duties of all Christians never cease, for we are to be full time Christians. Every contact we have with others, every attitude, every conversation, every letter, every deed, every greeting says something to others. Since the use technology, email messages, facebook, Link, or Twitter, etc. are means to reach out to spread the *good news* of the Gospel.

I remember as a child, going fishing with my father and catching fish. Sometimes I would have to cast the smaller or baby fish back in the lake, because they were too small to be skinned. Of course, this was disappointing to me, after my efforts to bait the hook with a worm and my efforts weren't rewarded by my catch.

Fishing for Souls is different, because Jesus said in *Mark 10:13-15, "And they brought young children to him, that he should them; and his disciples rebuked those that brought them. But when Jesus saw it, he was much displeased, and he said unto them, Suffer the little children to come unto me, and forbid them not; for of such is the kingdom of God. Verily I say unto you, Whosoever shall not receive the kingdom of God as a little child, he shall not enter therein."*

We may be the only example of Christianity that some have ever seen. We, as believers, are all here to advance the cause of Jesus Christ, and, as such, are all "missionaries" wherever He leads us—even if it is no farther than the four walls of a sickroom. Our "mission field" is all the unsaved people with whom we come in contact. Each one of them is looking for something which is unfulfilled in his life. May we give him bread, and not a stone; and may we love each to Christ.

Chapter 8

WITNESSING, the Work to Soul Winning

(Part I)

INTRODUCTION: In reducing soul winning to its most simple form, we have five basic verses which have proven. This study will show you how to use these verses in winning either Jews or Gentiles.

John 20:31 – Key to the Bible
"But these are written, that ye might believe that Jesus is the Christ, the Son of God; and that believing ye might have life through His name."

If the person believes that Jesus is the Son of God, congratulate him, and then ask, "Since believing, have you received God's gift of eternal life?" If he doesn't understand, it is evident that he has not received Christ. You can move to the next verse by saying, "Let me explain. There is a wall between every person and God. This wall is sin."

Romans 3:23 – All Have Sinned
"For all have sinned, and come short of the glory of God." Continue with your prospect by saying, "This verse says everyone has sinned." That takes in the very best people so it would certainly mean you and me, wouldn't it? Yes, it would. (Once sin is admitted, move to the next verse.)

Romans 6:23 – Penalty and Gift
"For the wages of sin is death; but the gift of God is eternal life through Jesus Christ our Lord." After showing the person this verse, you can explain: This word death means separation from God forever in hell or, in other words, death of the soul. Just as a man receives wages for working, God pays wages to people for sinning. When we understand this, add, aren't you glad the verse doesn't end with death? Look at the second part again. God offers us the gift of eternal life. It's so valuable that you can't work for it or pay for it. That's why it has to be gift. Your part is to accept it.

John 3:16 – Individual Importance
"For God so loved the world, that he gave his only begotten Son, that whosoever believeth in him, should not perish, but have everlasting life." Do you know how important you are to God? Then quote John 3:16, inserting that person's name. When you ask him who "whosoever" means he will probably answer, "Anybody." Agree and say it means you also.

Chapter 8

(Part II)

INTRODUCTION: The preceding lesson covered the first four verses from (John 20:31, Romans 3:23, Romans 6:23 and John 3:16) of a simple five-point plan that has proven effective in winning both Jews and Gentiles to Christ as presented for your study. Part II will include the final verse and basic convert follow-through.

Revelation 3:20 – Decision
"Behold I stand at the door, and knock; if any man hear my voice and open the door, I will come in to him and will sup with him, and he with me."

It is now time to apply the clincher. Let me show you how easy it is for you to have God's gift of eternal life. Using the verse, explain that this is Jesus speaking to him and that His voice is the Bible. What does Christ say He will do it if you open your life to Him?

He says He will come in. Now ask the contact if he would like to ask God to forgive his sins and accept Jesus as his Messiah or Savior. If he answers," Yes", you are ready to pray.

Forming a Simple Prayer
"That if thou shalt confess with thy mouth the Lord Jesus, and shalt believe in thine heart that God raised him from the dead, thou shalt be saved. For with the heart man believeth unto righteousness; and with the mouth confession is made unto salvation." Romans 10:9 and 10

In most cases, the person will not know how to pray so you must form the words and ask him to pray from his own heart. Here is a good simple prayer for the convert to follow, pausing after each phrase:

Dear Heavenly Father, I know that I am a sinner—Thank you for sending Jesus to die on the cross for me—Forgive me of all my sins. Wash my heart with His blood—I now accept Jesus into my heart right this minute—Thank you, Father—He is now in my heart—I have eternal life, in Jesus' name, Amen.

After Prayer
Now ask the person the three questions: Whom did you invite into your life? (Jesus) What did He take away? ("All my sins") where will you spend eternity someday? ("In heaven") The answers to all three questions should be clearly given by the new convert.. Work with the convert until all doubt is gone and there is a "know-so-answer."

Find out if he or she has a Bible and, if not, give a New Testament and make an appointment for your next visit.

Colossians 4:6 Amplified
"Let your speech at all times be gracious (pleasant and winsome), seasoned [as it were] with salt, [so that you may never be at a loss] to know how you ought to answer anyone [who puts a question to you]."

Chapter 8

WITNESSING, the Work to Soul Winning
The Excuses and How to Eliminate Rejections

Understanding the Basics to Soul Winning:
It is my opinion that there have been more *excuses* than *reasons* for the lack of evangelistic opportunities to the winning of souls in our churches today. Three common that seem to standout are: The *Excuse of Intimidation or Rejection*, The *Excuse of Ignorance*, and The *Excuse of Indifference*.

The *Excuse of Intimidation or Rejection*
This excuse says: *"If I witness I will be rejected by my friends."*
　　　　　　　"They will laugh at me when I mention Christ."
　　　　　　　"I am too embarrassed to talk to others about Christ."
　　　　　　　"I am afraid to tell about my past and the difference Christ has made."
　　　　　　　"Others can say it better than I."
　　　　　　　"I am afraid that after sharing the individual will not accept Christ."
　　　　　　　"I don't know enough of God's Word."

The *Excuse of Ignorance*
This excuse says: *"I don't know how to get started when I attempt to witness."*
　　　　　　　"I don't know what to tell them once I do get started."
　　　　　　　"They may ask me a question I won't have the answer to."

The *Excuse of Indifference*
This excuse says: *"It is not my responsibility."*
　　　　　　　"We have a team at church assigned to evangelism, so I don't need to get involved."
　　　　　　　"That is the role of the pastor and those that have a passion to win souls."
　　　　　　　"I am too busy with other things to witness."
　　　　　　　"God didn't call me to be a preacher, evangelists or missionary."
　　　　　　　"Evangelism is not my gift."
　　　　　　　"People should come to church like I did. No one approached me."

None of the above excuses are reasons for any of us not to reach out to people that need God by the death, burial and resurrection of Jesus Christ through the power and authority of the Holy Spirit [Ghost] to become their Savior and Deliverer. John 10:10 says *"The thief cometh not, but for to steal, and to kill, and to destroy: I am come that they might have life, and that they might have it more abundantly."*

How to Eliminate All Excuses:
A Call or Mandate from God from scripture, *"All authority in heaven and earth has been given to me. Therefore go and make disciples of all nations, baptizing them in the name of the Father and of the Son and of the Holy Spirit [Ghost], and teaching them to obey everything I have commanded you. And surely I am with you always, to the end of the age."*

Chapter 8

WITNESSING, the Work to Soul Winning
The Excuses and How to Eliminate Rejections

"We have a team at church assigned to evangelism, so I don't need to get involved."

"That is the role of the pastor and those that have a passion to win souls."

"I am too busy with other things to witness."

"God didn't call me to be a preacher, evangelists or missionary."

"Evangelism is not my gift."

"People should come to church like I did. No one approached me."

None of the above excuses are reasons for any of us not to reach out to people that need God by the death, burial and resurrection of Jesus Christ through the power and authority of the Holy Spirit (Ghost) to become their Savior and Deliverer. John 10:10 says "The thief cometh not, but for to steal, and to kill, and to destroy: I am come that they might have life, and that they might have it more abundantly."

How to Eliminate All Excuses:

A Call or Mandate from God from scripture, "All authority in heaven and earth has been given to me. Therefore go and make disciples of all nations, baptizing them in the name of the Father and of the Son and of the Holy Spirit (Ghost), and teaching them to obey everything I have commanded you. And surely I am with you always, to the end of the age."

Understanding the Basics to Soul Winning

Part 2…There are three "Voices" of Truth that can break or stop the Excuse Barrier.
How to Eliminate All Excuses: Matthew 28:18 - 20

1. A Call from God…This is the voice of the Lord.
God tells us that…We have the RIGHT to share the gospel., (Verse 18)

> "And Jesus came and spoke unto them, saying, All power is given unto me in heaven and in earth."

God tells us that…We have the RESPONSIBILITY to share the gospel. (Verse 19)

> "Go ye therefore, and teach all nations, baptizing them in the name of the Father, and of the Son, and of the Holy Ghost:"

God tells us that…We have the REASON to share the gospel. (Verse 20)

> "Teaching them to observe all things whatsoever I have commanded you: and lo, I am with you always, even unto the end of the world. Amen."

2. Having Compassion from within us…This is the voice of love.
"But when he saw the multitude, he was moved with compassion on them, because they fainted, and were scattered abroad, as sheep having no shepherd." Matthew 9:36

It tells us to…See the need with our eyes and Feel the need with our hearts!

3. A Cry from Beneath or Hell…Think of the alternative. This is the voice of the lost!
Luke 16:22-28 saying, "And it came to pass, that the beggar died, and was carried by the angels into Abraham's bosom: the rich man also died, and was buried; And in hell

CHAPTER 9

Qualifications for Fishers of Men

St. Mark 1:17

"And Jesus said unto them, Come ye after me, and I will make you to become fishers of men."

Personal Qualifications for Evangelism:

The fact has been stressed that all Christians, followers of Christ, are commissioned to undertake this great task of evangelism; however, this does not indicate that personal evangelism is to be classified is to be classified as unskilled labor, and that no qualifications are needed—this is quite the contrary. It is important or vital that we become prepared in every way possible for the work that we have been called to do, rather one on one or corporately as a church. Listed are suggested characteristics we need to develop and mature in the ways of the Lord.

1. **Assurance of Your Own Salvation (II Timothy 1:12 Amplified; I John 5:13)**

   "And this is why I am suffering as I do. Still I am not ashamed, for I know (perceive, have knowledge of, and am acquainted with) Him Whom I have believed (adhered to and trusted in relied on), and I am [positively] persuaded that He is able to guard and keep that which has been entrusted to me and which I have committed [to Him] until that day." II Timothy 1:12 Amplified

"These things have I written unto you that believe on the name of the Son of God; that ye may know that ye have eternal life; and that ye may believe on the name of the Son of God." I John 5:13

Whoever undertakes this work must have assurance himself of the gospel which he proclaims. If you were witnessing to someone about the wonderful Gospel of Jesus Christ and that person asked you, "How do you know that you are really saved, "What would be your answer? Could you reply with a resounding, "Yes?" Could you answer with the same affirmative that the Apostle Paul wrote in II Timothy 1:12?

If you do not have this blessed assurance, you need to search God's Word and meditate on it until you know that you have life eternal. There are many souls longing to find someone longing to find someone who can speak with deep conviction and authority about the unshakeable assurance of salvation through Jesus Christ.

Remember, a doubting hold on your faith produces weak evangelism, but unshakeable hold on your faith produces power evangelism.

2. A Good Working Knowledge of the Scriptures (II Timothy 2:15)

Anyone who desires to be a successful witness must learn to be skilled in the use of the Bible. You *do not* have to know the entire Bible, but particular scriptures should be memorized, especially regarding salvation. Other knowledge is no doubt valuable, but a working knowledge of the Bible is of utmost importance and is ongoing. For it is through personal application of the Scriptures that spiritual life is developed.

The Bible, and the Bible only, shows the way of salvation, exposes heresies, and dispels objections and excuses. Consequently the soul-winner must be a student of the Word if he is to know success.

3. A Soul Winner Must Remain "Dressed for Battle"

"Wherefore take unto you the whole armour of God; that ye may be able to withstand in the evil day, and having done all, to stand. Stand therefore, having your loins girt about with truth, and having on the breastplate of righteousness; And your feet shod with preparation of the gospel of peace; Above all, taking the shield of faith, where-with ye shall be able to quench all the fiery darts of the wicked. And take the helmet of salvation, and the sword of the Spirit, which is the word of God: Praying always with all prayer and supplication in the Spirit, and watching thereunto with all perseverance and supplication for all saints" (Ephesians 6:13-18).

4. A Life of Prayer

Individuals must be led as to which direction to take and to whom he should speak to the appropriate time, but through prayer. How else can we receive direction, unless we are constantly acknowledging God through prayer?

"In all thy ways acknowledge him, and he shall direct thy paths." (Proverbs 3:6)

"And He spake a parable unto them to this end, that men ought always pray, and not faint;" (Luke 18:1)

"Pray without ceasing." (I Thessalonians 5:18)

Prayer opens the door for witnessing. We should ask God in prayer to prepare the soil of men heart so that they will be able to receive the seed of His Word. We must also pray that the person we are witnessing to will be liberated from the power of Satan and that blindness from the truth will be removed from his spiritual eyes. We must pray that God will give boldness and courage to speak for Him. Prayer, then, is definitely a must if we want to be a successful soul-winner.

5. Exercise Tact in Your Approach

Webster defines *tact* as "a sense of the right thing to say or do without offering; skill in dealing with people." We need to know how to approach people with the gospel.

If the worker does not have a lovingly tactful approach, they often spoil the work for which they are concerned for. Our approach to the unsaved should never be a "sanctified conceit." We are never to point to ourselves, but to someone who is above, Jesus Christ. We ask others to be like us only in our faith. Paul, as a prisoner, said to the king, "I wish that you were as I am," but he added, "except for my limitations." In essence, he was saying, even though I have many limitations, I am a personal witness to the wonderful things God has done in my life. An attitude of this kind takes away offensiveness from our witness, and allows us to give answers to every man for the reason of the hope we have with meekness and fear.

6. Patience

"Therefore, my beloved brethren, be ye steadfast, immoveable, always abounding in the work of the Lord, forasmuch as ye know that your labour is not in vain in the Lord." (I Corinthians 15:58)

"Recalling unceasingly before our God and Father your work energized by faith and service motivated by love and unwavering hope in [the return of] our Lord Jesus Christ (the Messiah)." (I Thessalonians 1:3, Amplified)

"But thou, O man of God, flee these things; and follow after righteousness, godliness, faith, love, patience, meekness." (I Timothy 6:11)

Results from the work of evangelism may sometimes be discouraging when one does not see immediate results. Therefore, the personal worker must possess the virtue of patience. Just as the fisherman sitting on the bank with his pole, waiting patiently for the fish to nibble at the bait. The fishermen in the Bible would wait through the night, if necessary, to fill their nets with fish. Patience, endurance, determination, and persistence are characteristics that any soul winner should possess as they mature in patience.

7. Love for People

"This is my commandment, that ye love one another, as I have loved you." (John 15:12)

Greater love hath no man than this, that a man lay down his life for his friends." (John 15:12, 13)

"And we have known and believed the love that God hath to us; God is love; and he that dwelleth in God, and God in him." (I John 4:16)

8. Possess the Power of God

"But ye shall receive power, after that the Holy Ghost is come upon you: and ye shall be witnesses unto me both in Jerusalem, and in all Judea, and in Samaria, and unto the uttermost part of the earth." (Acts 1:8)

It is with this principle in mind that the soul-winner must pursue his task. Really caring about the whole of an individual and what happens to him is essential. The people we approach will sense it if our main aim is to increase the number of members in our church rather than a genuine concern for their souls. While a warmhearted friendliness of love is not the only aspect of evangelism, it paves the way for others. Love is one of the most powerful ways to dispel resentment and opposition. It is the credentials people look for those who wish to witness to them about the good news of Jesus Christ. Therefore, make love your aim! *Let's go fishing!*

"And daily in the temple, and in every house, they ceased not to teach and preach Jesus Christ." (Acts 5:42)

Just as one prepares himself for his natural job and duties in life, how much more should he prepare for the greatest and most rewarding task in the world, the art of soul winning? The qualities shared are not strenuous or require great exertion, but a consistent effort to *". . . do the work of an evangelist, make full proof of thy ministry." (II Timothy 4:5)*

In Summary

"The fruit of righteous is a tree of life; and he that wins souls is wise." (Proverbs 11:30)

1. Soul winning is the life-line of the church:

   B. *"Where there is no vision, the people perish; . . ."*
      (Proverbs 29:18)
   C. *Personal work can be done where preaching cannot.*

4. Reproduction or fruit bearing

   A. Without the reproduction of other Christians our gospel would die in our generation. [The human cycle is that we reproduce ourselves.]
   B. *"Ye have not chosen me, but I have chosen you, and ordained you, that ye should go and bring forth fruit, . . ."*
      (John 15:16)

3. God will hold us responsible.

   A. *Am I my brother's keeper? (Genesis 4:9; Ezekiel 33:6-10; Mark 1:17)*
   B. *"I must work the works of him that sent me, while it is day: the night cometh, when no man can work."*

3. To live victoriously as soul-winners, we must *pray* to stay and *fast* to last.

A. "Pray without ceasing." (I Thessalonians 5:18)

B. "Consecrate a fast, Call a sacred assembly; Gather the elders and all the inhabitants of the land into the house of the Lord your God, and cry out to the Lord." (Joel 1:14)

C. "However, this kind does not go out except by prayer and fasting." (Matthew 17:21)

D. "Nay, in all these things we are more than conquerors through him that loved us." (Romans 8:37)

5. Qualifications

A. Love for souls
"A new commandment I give unto you, That ye love one another; as I have loved you, that ye also love one another; By this shall all men know that ye are my disciples, if ye have love one to another." (John 13:34–35)

"For the love of Christ controls and urges and impels us, because we are of the opinions and conviction that [if] One died for all, then all died; And He died for all, so that all those who live might live no longer to and for themselves, but to and for Him Who died and was raised again for their sake." (II Corinthians 5:14–15, Amplified)

B. Personal experienced knowledge of Salvation.
"So whoever cleanses himself [from what is ignoble and unclean, who separates himself from contact with contaminating and corrupting influences] will [then himself] be a vessel set apart and useful for honorable and noble purposes, consecrated and profitable to the Master, fit and ready for any good work." (II Timothy 3:21, Amplified)

"We know [absolutely] that anyone born of God does not [deliberately and knowingly] practice committing sin, but the One, Who was the begotten of God carefully watches over and protects him [Christ's divine presence within him preserves him against the evil], and the wicked one does not lay hold (get a grip) on him or touch [him]." (I John 5:18, Amplified)

C. Infilling of the Holy Ghost (Spirit)
Jesus said, "But ye shall receive power after that the Holy Ghost is come upon you: and ye shall be witnesses unto me both in Jerusalem, and in all Judea, and in Samaria, and unto the uttermost part of the earth." (Acts 1:8)

D. Practical knowledge of the Bible
"Study to show thyself approved unto God, a workman that needeth not be ashamed, rightly dividing the word of truth." (II Timothy 2:15)

W—Witness out of Love

I—Inform what the Bible says about the new life

T—Testify of Jesus' goodness in your life.

N—Newness in Him

E—Eternal life is promised

S—Salvation immediately

S—Sanctification; made Holy; set apart for the Master's use

CHAPTER 10

The Ways, Means, and Methods for Effective Evangelism

Listed are suggestive ways to win souls, rather traditional or contemporary methods. Some can be used as one on one tactics or cooperate outreach techniques directed by the pastor through the use of the evangelism departments.

- Have a definite time to go.
- Be soul conscious by talking to any one at any time that contact is made.
- Witness two by two with tracts.
- Ask attention getting questions: "If you died now, do you know that you would go to Heaven?"
- Break out into teams, so spreading out into the community is covered.
- Pass out tracts wherever possible with name and address of church available.
- "Prayer Combat Raids", use the church (vans) to travel to certain areas of community to pray openly and move to another location.
- Use youth drill teams throughout the community to draw attention in the work of evangelism.
- Pass out Bibles, Daily Breads, and Prayer Books in institutions that will allow individuals to become recipients.

- Conduct outdoor services where permitted. "Taking IT to the Streets!"
- Use the Word of God as validation to prove "it is written" what God makes available for every individual for eternity.

Personal Preparation:

1. Claim the Holy Spirit's fullness before reaching out.
2. Be compassionate and passionate when sharing the message or testimony of Salvation.
3. Be a "Good Listener", allow your *heart* to respond to the hearer of your message or testimony.
4. Let your approach be handled with sensitivity.
5. Be clean. Be neat. Be courageous. Be determined. Be consistent. Be approachable. Be open. Be honest.

Evangelism is the mandate for church growth since the Book of Acts when the wfirst church was started through the spreading of the gospel. Numerical as well as spiritual growth result from evangelism in church ministry. Without evangelism the church program becomes routine and unproductive.

It is the work or outreach that gives balance to personal and church wide evangelism for each believer. Although all believers may not have the gift of evangelism, all should be able to witness to their faith in Christ and have a part in the church's evangelistic effort. Although the message of the gospel has not changed, there are different strategies in every generation which proves effective in reaching the lost for Christ. Rather than holding to traditional methods because "that's the way it has always been done,"

Christians should be seeking to examine new approaches and incorporate them into their evangelism strategy.

Living in the 21st Century, seemingly has released a wide range of issues that define sin in every sense of imaginations. It gives the appearance that everything imaginable has "come out of the closet." The internet has updated our ability to reach out, rather for the good or the bad. As Christians, we must do our part to not fall behind to witness and expand the work of evangelism through any means possible.

This chapter will attempt to describe various evangelistic strategies that from personal (one on one) to reaching the masses [church evangelistic programs] to effectively fulfill The Great Commission to *"Go ye therefore, and teach all nations, baptizing them in the name of the Father, and of the Son, and of the Holy Ghost;" Matthew 28:19* and *Mark 1:17 "..., Come ye after me, and I will make you to become fishers of men."*

Included are places, events and ways that were implemented, from the vision of the late Bishop Marvin C. Pryor, as pastor of Victorious Believers Ministries Church of God in Christ in Saginaw, Michigan. I was honored and privileged to serve as director for evangelism for the local church and jurisdiction.

1. Revival Services
2. Street Services
3. Tent Services
4. Park Services
5. Children Ministry Outreach
6. Evangelism Skits (Church and offsite locations)

7. Tract and Flier Distribution

8. Mail Contact

9. Campus Ministry

10. Prison Ministry

11. Cell Ministry

12. Contemporary Classes/Sunday school Department

Listed are different styles and methods of evangelism. These would include, but are not limited to, the following:

Styles and Methods of Evangelism

Proclamational: includes pulpit preaching, teaching, crusade evangelism, conferences, revival meetings, seminars, rallies, speaking in front of groups

Confrontational: includes sharing with people you don't know in public places, or going door-to-door attempting to visit with people in their homes

Relational: includes lifestyle, conversational, interpersonal, and friendship evangelism

Power: includes praying for people you meet and know for the needs they have in their lives, to see God's power and then respond to Him in faith

Intellectual: includes biblical apologetics, defending Christianity and the Bible with logic, science, and reason

Testimonial: includes sharing your story with others how you came to believe in Christ, what God has done, and what He is currently doing in your life

Invitational: includes inviting others to your church or evangelistic event

Service: includes serving the needs of others in the name of Christ so they will see Christ in your actions

Personal: includes what an individual does to share Christ with others

Church: includes what a congregation does corporately in programs, events, and strategies to share Christ with others

Prayer: include prayer walking, prayer journeys, van drives through neighborhoods praying, intercessory prayer on behalf of the felt needs of the lost, talking to God about before talking to people about God

Shut-Ins: include prayer, Bible study, testimonies, worship and praise, teaching and preaching continual during a set time periodically

Technical Methods:

- Technology used since Pandemic 2020
  Email
  Facebook
  Zoom
  Messages

       Messenger

       Twitter

       YouTube

- Cell Phones
- Cable TV
- iPods
- GPS Tracking Systems
- Electronic Tablets

We must never stop doing evangelism. Christians use faulty reasoning or excuses to justify their lack of involvement in a lifestyle of evangelism. Some churches have become dependent upon a certain group that is identified to serve, but it is the responsibility for every member to do their part to win the lost to Christ. We must never compromise the message with whatever method is used. We must never lose our focus to live and share the Gospel message.

The Evangelistic Approach: "He that Win souls, must be wise!"

How to Witness to atheists, agnostics, and evolutionists:

Atheists:
Who are they?

1. Atheists do not believe in the existence of any god.
2. Atheists usually believe in the process of evolution.
3. Atheists usually do not accept the concept of an afterlife.
4. Atheists hold to some sort of moral code.

   Note: This is where atheists are inconsistent. Although they don't believe in a moral lawgiver (God), they do believe in morals (i.e., "murder is wrong"). However, if there is no God, there are no morals!

How to witness to them?

There are some preconceived notions people have about atheists. Many of these have made us reluctant to reach out to them.

1. *Atheists are more intelligent.* An atheist's ability to articulate their views is evidence *of intelligence but it doesn't mean they know all the facts.* We need to be equally *prepared and able to articulate our faith and the evidence that led us to believe.*

2. *Atheists are uncaring.* Atheists are often very generous and caring. Many will contribute generously to humanitarian causes. Also, we cause another barrier to witnessing for Christ if we assume that all atheists are uncaring regarding others. Let the *love* of God shine through our hearts so it will draw and not cause them to reject the message.

3. *Atheists are viciously anti-God.* All atheists aren't alike. Some are on a "mission" to convert others to accept what they believe about religion, especially the teachings about God. They are not all unified, teaming with the ACLU, and trying to remove the Ten Commandments from our government buildings or prayer from our public schools. Some are just simply someone have chosen not to believe in God and doesn't want people *forcing* others to believe in him. We, as Christians must not become confrontational in our approach, but gentle and prayerfully patient in our presentation.

4. *Atheists are beyond help.* Never give up praying and hoping that if you aren't the individual to *win* them to Christ, that God will have others available.

A Strategy That Works:

Sadly, most atheists believe Christians are irrelevant, uneducated, naïve, or inconsistent hypocrites. It is absolutely that you strive to be transparent and consistent in your faith lifestyle. Many of us say one thing while witnessing and live contrary to what we teach. Once credibility is established, they will be intrigued and curious to find out why such a person would believe in God.

Pray before approach. Enlist the right people for help. Expose the atheist to God's Word!

Agnostics:

Who are they?

1. Agnostics vary from person to person in their belief system.
2. Agnostics believe no one can know God if God exists.
3. Agnostics hold to some sort of moral code.

   Note: The word "agnostic" literally means "one without knowledge."

Here are various questions to ask an atheist/agnostic:

- *"If there is no God, then shouldn't people be able to do what they want, even murder?"*
- *"If there is no God, then how can you explain a human's conscience (sense of good and evil)?"*
- *If Jesus Christ wasn't God, then who was He?"*

For example: *"Have you seen or noticed a beautiful painting on a wall? It did not just suddenly appear! An artist made a plan and then took his time, creativity, and energy to paint the picture. In the same way, something much more vast, beautiful, and complicated than a painting—like people—requires Someone much more creative, strategic, and powerful than an artist. That Someone is God!"*

Included is a list of false doctrines. It is not necessary to be educated in detail or an expert but informed enough to guide your approach. You can access information from the internet or other reference books.

CHAPTER 11

Closing the Back Door, *Follow Up*

"Closing the Back Door" is a phrase that defines the work by any church involved in keeping those who are won to Christ by the efforts of evangelism. It is not enough to lead an individual or masses to repentance; but mentoring or assigning a *matured* saint to assist the new convert in their early walk in the Lord is needed. The purpose in this chapter is to suggest ways that were practiced at VBM, under the direction of the pastor, the late Bishop Marvin C. Pryor, as a model for other ministries to follow.

Mentoring:

A new convert is vulnerable in their early stage of understanding the new life in Christ Jesus.

It is important to follow up with the convert after their conversion. It is necessary to assure them that accepting of the Lord in their life at the altar or if witnessed to one on one; wasn't an emotional or just being caught up in the moment happening, but a real genuine experience!

There are collective efforts to disciplining or training someone how to live differently from their failed past. Even though the Bible says in *II Corinthians 5:17, "Therefore, if any man be in Christ, he is a new creature, old things have passed away; behold all things have become new."* To understand what this new life in Christ takes time and the assistance of others. Of course, new converts should be encouraged to attend church services regularly, after their conversion and membership. Someone is needed to partner with the "new babe in Christ." The work involved in follow up is characterized in several forms; such as being available to encourage participation, help the new convert discover their Spiritual gifts, provide answers to any questions, as well as advice or suggestions and to help the new member connect to the pastor. The purpose of the follow up ministry; is to assure that in time, the new convert will eventually become confident in their new life and become a committed to the Lord through the efforts of the church. As they mature, they too, will become a mentor and assist others, as they were in the beginning of their *walk in Christ.* The mentor is not seeking for a "best friend" but being as the Bible states, *"my brother's keeper."*

We can't take for granted or assume everyone has some kind of church background, when they become members. We are now living in a time where many that are being witnessed to have little or no history of church upbringing. It became necessary to identify mature saints to connect and make themselves available to as new members at VBM. It was important to recognize those of us that had been faithful and understood the vision by the pastor. We were committed not only in attendance, using our Spiritual gifts, but supported by the giving of tithes and offerings. New members don't always understand the "church jargon" commonly spoken in church. Having someone assigned to serve as a mentor, helps eliminate misunderstandings and misinterpretations for the mentees.

Mentoring also gives the new convert a prayer partner, so that communicating to God out loud becomes easier to do on a consistent basis.

New Members' Classes:

First, it is important that new members need formal instructions for understanding the operation or church programming and a general overview of the Bible. I was honored to serve as the assistant teacher of the New Members' Class, under the direction of the pastor, Bishop Marvin C. Pryor. Teaching the foundation to holiness, doctrine, VBM ministries, and assisting to help new members to discover their Spiritual gifts were the purpose for instituting this set time of learning. It also provided an opportunity for the new member to have one on one instructing time with the pastor. New Members were able to have personal time with the pastor's wife, Evangelist Ruth C. Pryor. In my opinion, this class caused members to adjust the ministry and become actively involved in the church. The majority that attended all of the sessions, were able to transitioned into other ministries of the church and yet remain involved at the VBM church. Of course, when he was elevated to the office of a bishop, it was vital that new members understand what this role would mean to the ministry of the local church.

Secondly, these classes became a part of the Sunday School Department schedule. Therefore, by having students forming the habit of attending classes weekly, made transitioning to an assigned class easy. Pastor Pryor made sure that he presented himself as personal with the new members during these sessions. He took the effort to call each by their name, and from reviewing the membership application, shared something about each. It made new members realize that who they were was important to him as their pastor.

On a personal note, assisting Pastor Pryor to instruct about God's Word, informed foundational lessons about the ministry, and to assisting discovering their Spiritual gifts, was impacting upon my life. The confidence that Pastor Pryor entrusted in me was an esteemed honor. Selfishly, it allowed me the opportunity to be up close and personal with my brother, pastor and bishop.

Provision of Tools:

New Members are need books and materials very early in their *new walk* in Christ. The church should be in position to assist or provide, so new converts can begin equipped. VBM provided Bibles, instructional materials in the form of bible lessons, new beginning book, and outlines on the various ministries of the local church.

Suggested tools that will help study the Bible: the Holy Bible (KJV, Amplified, NIV), Bible Dictionary, Concordance, recorded messages with the use of tapes, DVDs, and use of internet.

The ministry provided information to Christian bookstores, so new members could select books of choice. I recommend *A Guidebook for Growing Believers... The New Life, The Start of Something Wonderful* by Dave Williams, published by Decapolis Publishing, P.O. Box 80825, Lansing, Michigan 48908-0825.

I applaud ministries that have implemented new members' classes, so that formal instruction with the use of the Bible and materials are made available.

Cell Groups:

Placing new members with a smaller group of the church became common practice at VBM. The smaller groups were labeled as cell groups. This ministry could be identified as the *lifeline* of the VBM church. Each cell team would make direct contact with the individuals on their list. The team would get involved in social activities outside of the church setting. An individual could be guaranteed that a set group from the local church would visit families during the time of illnesses, funerals, and hospitals visitations. The leaders of each cell team would make sure members were informed of services, activities and cancellations too. Pastor Pryor could feel good that he knew that there were assigned groups who would assist him by being available to make contact to every VBM member on his behalf.

Ministry Publications:

VBM members could receive the publication of *The Spirit of Victory Newsletter.* The publication of this newsletter stretched throughout the United States, as well to the members of the congregation. It was another way that Pastor Pryor could connect with the congregation on various topics.

Evangelist Ruth, First Lady of VBM, was known for sending cards and letters to members. She didn't discriminate. New and established members could receive something in the mail to let them know how important their membership to Victorious

Believers Ministries meant. All of these were ways to *follow up,* so that every member could know their presence and involvement was important to the growth, development and success to the ministry. Even though some strategies have been changed or updated. Bishop Pryor is no longer available to guide; Pastor Christopher V. Pryor and Sister Kenyatta are making sure that every member is connected to the vision.

CHAPTER 12

Revival Under the Tent
Powerful, Fresh, and Anointed!

"Taking It to the Streets!" by Elder Mel A. Pryor

In Memory of the Late Elder Mel A. Pryor

"Go out into the highways and hedges and compel them to come in, that my house may be filled (Luke 14:23)," was the driving force of our annual community tent revival this summer. It was Powerful, Fresh and Anointed! The saints danced, shouted and rejoiced under the big tent—good old-fashioned church! It was all about souls-winning the lost to Jesus Christ.

Once again, VBM (Victorious Believers Ministries) joined forces with Believers around the Saginaw community to launch an attack on Satan's camp. Although this inner city battleground is known for crime and violence, we were armed with weapons of mass destruction (The Sword of the Spirit, Prayer and Holy Ghost Power) to defeat Satan. Testimonies of salvation, healing and deliverance were shared during this week of open air evangelistic services. Youth and adults lined the sidewalk waving colorful banners and signs to alert the passersby on wheels and feet to come experience a wonderful new life in Christ.

Our guest revivalist of the week, Pastor Zachary Williamson of Saginaw, along with the anointed men and women of God of VBM brought forth the gospel with simplicity, conviction and power! The reinvigorating music and singing (Brother Sidney Oliver as Minister of Music and Elder Christopher Pryor as praise leader), penetrated the atmosphere across the city blocks.

Once again, reporters from every area television network and county newspaper were led to capture the excitement on multiple occasions throughout the week at the noon and evening services.

The resounding question was, "Why are you here?" Our spiritual outpouring was complemented by an outpouring of clothing and food give-away to those in need. The love of God was evident in Word and deed. The church must come outside of its walls and take the gospel message to the streets. Sinners must know that we care and to the utmost Jesus saves. If the church isn't good enough for everybody, then it is good enough for anybody.

Jesus Christ died for ALL!

Footnote:

Bishop Pryor would annually lead the evangelistic team and the members of VBM to conduct services at noon and in the evening. He was an active participant. As you view the photos, they capture his love for getting out among the people to show the love of God to the community. It didn't matter about his title as a bishop, former educator, but his willingness to let everyone attending that being an ambassador for Christ was the priority of his existence.

The evangelism team, under the direction of yours truly, would prepare for the annual tent revivals; by making sure that every ministry from the local church were involved, equipment needed and setup workers were in place and fliers spread throughout city and surrounding cities. Pastors attended and participated; it was another opportunity to show the community, regardless of denominations, race, greed or color, we had a single mind of purpose—to fight Satan!

Bishop Pryor with former Mayor Wilmer Ham

Bishop Pryor at the podium, while Evang.
Carol encourage the saints to praise the Lord!

Pastor Zachary Williamson, Guest Evangelist, preaches with passion Bishop Pryor is being interviewed by Saginaw's television station; while the adults and youth wave banners and signs compelling any passing by to join us.

My final chapter includes the photos, flier and outline preparation for tent services from the past at Victorious Believers Ministries. It was my responsibility, serving as the Director of Evangelism, to plan a week of services offsite. It involved a faithful team of workers to organize every area. Individuals were assigned to serve as contact.

Programming: Bishop Marvin C. and Evangelist Ruth C. Pryor
Invite surrounding churches
Invite mayor and city officials
Music ministry , praise and worship team
Abs tent, chairs and lighting
Mobile rental sign
Sound board with microphones, stands, and speakers
Generator(s)
Clothing and food giveaway: VBM mission's department
VBM minute men (set up/break down daily) and security
VBM banner ministry
Big truck rental
VBM vans (2)
Street sign
Johnny on the spot (2)
Parking lots
Hospitality
Nurses' guild
Media: television and radio stations/interviews
Prayer vigils
Ministerial team: elders and missionaries
Altar follow-up workers
Drill team

Children ministry

Police department patrols

Neighborhood outreach (businesses and private homes)

Photography

Tracks

Old Fashioned Tent Reviva

2 Powerful Services Daily

Monday July 14th thru Friday July 18th

Service Monday begins at 7:00 p.m.

Services : Tuesday - Friday
12:00 NOON & 7:00 p.m.

(Location of Services)
1222 E. Genesee & Burt, Saginaw, MI 48601
(Next to Food Value Supermarket)

Healing

Victorious Believers Ministries ; 624 S. Outer Dr. Saginaw, MI 48601
989-755-7692 ext. 5
Bishop Marvin C. Pryor, Pastor

Deliveranc

Preaching   **Singing**

Salvation

COMMUNITY Tent Revival

2 POWER SERVICES DAILY

MONDAY – JUNE 27 -thru-FRIDAY – JULY 1

Salvation
Deliverance
Praise Dancn

12:00 NOON & 7:00 P.M.
(Location of Services)
1122 E. Genesee Burt
Saginaw, MI 48601
(Next to Tony's Food Value Supermarket)

Preaching
Singing
Music

Free Food & Clothing Give-Away

Victorious Believers Ministries
624 S. Outer Dr. Saginaw, MI 48601
(989) 755-7692 Ext. 5
Bishop Marvin C. Pryor, Pastor

Healing

Victorious Believers Ministries
Old Fashioned Tent Revival
Songs Listing

1. Come On, Don't You Want to Go?
2. Come to Jesus
3. Have You Tried Jesus?
4. He Brought Me Out
5. Hold to God's Unchanging Hand
6. I Have Decided to Follow Jesus
7. I Surrender All
8. I Was Sinking Deep in Sin
9. I'd Rather Have Jesus
10. I'm a Soldier
11. I'm So Glad Jesus Lifted Me
12. I've Decided to Make Jesus My Choice
13. I've Got a Feeling
14. If You Call on Jesus
15. Is My Name Written There?
16. Jesus Loves the Little Children
17. Jesus Saves
18. Just Like Fire
19. Let Jesus Fix It for You
20. Lift Him Up
21. Lord, I Want to Go
22. Love Lifted Me
23. My Soul Says, "Yes"
24. Praise Him! Praise Him!
25. Room at the Cross
26. Since Jesus Came into My Heart
27. Take The Lord Along with You
28. There Is Power in the Blood

Bishop Marvin C. and Evangelist Ruth C. Pryor (First Lady) of Victorious Believers Ministries COGIC Saginaw, Michigan Jurisdiction Prelate of Southwestern Michigan #3 Church of God in Christ, Inc.

AUTHOR'S AUTOBIOGRAPHY

"I am crucified with Christ; nevertheless I live; yet not I, but
Christ lives in me: and the life which I now live in the flesh I live
by the faith of the Son of God, who loved me, and gave himself me."
—Galatians 2:20

Dr. Carol J. Pryor was born in Jackson, Michigan, by parents who served God faithfully until God called them to their reward. Carol was the eight of nine children; one of which who died as an infant. All eight children were trained in Godly principles. Carol is a 3rd generation Church of God in Christ, reared in the disciplines of this Christian denomination. Her grandfather established one of the first Church of God in Christ in southern Illinois during 1917. The church was later renamed the Pryor Memorial Church of God in Christ in Villa Ridge, Illinois; fondly named Pryor Town. The church is celebrating more than a hundred years of existence.

Carol is a former educator, retired from the Flint School District in Flint, Michigan with a degree in in education, teaching more than twenty-five years. Since moving to the city of Spring, Texas in 2007, she earned a master's degree and advanced to obtain a doctorate from Wilmington, North Carolina. In 2011, she received certification as a Christian Counselor from the International Christian Institute in Houston, Texas.

Evangelist Carol received her license as an Evangelist Missionary from the Southwest Michigan Jurisdiction. She felt honored and blessed to have had her license renewed in 1996 by her brother, who served as her pastor and bishop; the late Bishop Marvin C. Pryor of Southwest Michigan #3 in Saginaw, Michigan.

It was Bishop Pryor, who also appointed her the first female to serve as the president for the evangelism department of that jurisdiction in the Church of God in Christ.

Evangelist Carol is yet connected to Victorious Believers Ministries Church of God in Christ in Saginaw, Michigan; where her nephew, Supt. Christopher V. Pryor, serves as the pastor, since the death of his father in 2010. For nearly twenty-five years serving under the leadership of Bishop Pryor, she served in vital roles at the local ministry and jurisdiction to assist the fulfilling of his vision to achieve "Excellence in Holiness!" Some of those positions at the local church were, assistant teacher to Pastor Pryor for the New Members' Class, Director of Evangelism; which included coordinating the prison ministry; outdoor events; yearly tent revival services; and altar ministry training.

For sixteen years, Evangelist Carol served as the Vocal Praise leader for Victorious Christian Women in Flint, Michigan. VCW served as an annual women's conference; that involved women from a wide range of denominations gathered for a weekend of worship services; classes and fellowship. This conference attracted women from other states and contributed to the Spiritual growth and introduction of many women as known speakers throughout the United States. Evangelist Carol founded a ministry named

INREACH; where she combined education, experiences, spiritual incite and history of past practices to form:

I—Intercessory Prayer training

N—New Beginning Restoration development

R—Revivals (conducting Old Fashioned Revival Services)

E—Evangelism Outreach (include one on one, campus and prison Ministries)

A—Administration (Adjutancy, Altar Ministry and Armor Bearer training)

C—Church Protocol; and Christian Counselor

H—Harvest (Global Outreach opportunities)

Dr. Carol can be contacted by email, evangpryor@aol.com, to schedule opportunities regarding any of the above.

CPSIA information can be obtained
at www.ICGtesting.com
Printed in the USA
BVHW042201241022
649939BV00007B/8